Our Lady of Victory

Our Lady of Victory

The Saga of an African-American Catholic Community

Shirley Harris-Slaughter

iUniverse, Inc.

New York Lincoln Shanghai

Our Lady of Victory
The Saga of an African-American Catholic Community

iUniverse books may be ordered through booksellers or by contacting:

iUniverse
2021 Pine Lake Road, Suite 100
Lincoln, NE 68512
www.iuniverse.com
1-800-Authors (1-800-288-4677)

Because of the dynamic nature of the Internet, any Web addresses or links contained in this book may have changed since publication and may no longer be valid.

The views expressed in this work are solely those of the author and do not necessarily reflect the views of the publisher, and the publisher hereby disclaims any responsibility for them.

Photos by Dwight Cendrowski

ISBN: 978-0-595-43482-4 (pbk)
ISBN: 978-0-595-89668-4 (cloth)
ISBN: 978-0-595-87809-3 (ebk)

Printed in the United States of America

People will always have an opinion about what we say or do. That is why we live our lives according to the words of the Bible—God's opinion. Then we will not fret over the opinions of others.

(Unknown Author)

Contents

Acknowledgments

Special thanks to Ruth Green-Leonard for sharing your souvenir booklet, *A Church Closes—A Spirit Continues*. Special thanks to Richard E. Smith for your works, *Development of Our Lady of Victory* and *West Eight Mile*, which explore how the church and the community developed.

These individuals helped in many different ways on this project: John Fleming for historical input; Sr. Mary Elise for bringing us together; Roman Godzak, Archdiocese of Detroit for access to archives; Fr. Thomas Ebong for advice and input; Sr. Sharon Young for assistance and referrals to the Oblate Sisters of Providence Archives in Baltimore, Maryland, which led to Fr. Peter Hogan, a Josephite who enlightened me to their presence in the Detroit area; Rev. Mr. Hubert Sanders for unlimited access to Our Lady of Victory archives and those historical and priceless photos; Betty White-Palmer for providing a record of the Sodality Girls and assistance in identifying photos; Almeta Carruth-White for granting an interview (and Gloria Cook for bringing us together); Ona Harris and mother, Marcella Carter, for their interview, which enlightened me to the innovative Claude Carter; Madelene and Philip Fortier for the photos and memories (Philip, you are young, but you are an old soul); Foster Wilson II; and Marjorie Green for sharing your knowledge on the Knights of St. Peter Claver history.

In addition, I want to thank Naomi Anderson, Doris West, Mary Elizabeth Robinson, Mae Ruth Little, Jerry Rankin, Lorna Wilson-Thomas, Daisy Smith, Sarah Dargin-Ware, and Darlie Bouie for their invaluable help.

A special acknowledgment goes to Msgr. Ferdinand DeCneudt for providing photos and books for this project and for his enthusiastic support and confidence in me.

This book is dedicated to the memory of Washington and Lillie Leonard, Boyce Robinson Sr., Razz and Betty Flowers, Steve and Audrey Johnson, Foster and Earline Wilson Sr., Fred and Almeta Carruth, Luther Keith,

Our Lady of Victory

James Anderson, Bud Bouie, Helen Wilson, Alfred Cook, Mother Stella Marie, Martha Palms-Williams (my dear godmother), and my godfather, Thomas Cunningham, who was so inspiring. And also to Sarah McKenzie-Hilton who just recently passed away.

I dedicate this book to the memory of my dear mother, Joyce Winifred Burkes-Giles, a gifted poet, writer, and speaker, who was determined that her children receive a good education.

For those who are not mentioned, may God bless you for blazing the trail in your own way.

Foreword

This book by Shirley Slaughter gives us a bird's-eye view of the tension between the Catholic Church's legal authorities and black Catholic communities. Black Catholic parishes have faced considerable difficulties preserving their identities and traditions in a challenging environment.

There are no villains in this mix. The Catholic Church in America has also been victimized as she struggled to work through the complexities of mixed races and cultures. In the great migrations of the twentieth century came the Irish, the Italians, the Poles, the Germans, the Belgians, and others. European priests who came to the United States to shepherd their own nationals were now suddenly confronted with a dysfunctional society reeling from the remnants of slavery and institutionalized racism.

Shirley's book sheds considerable light on the life of one black Catholic community, Our Lady of Victory Mission, and its effort to survive and grow amid great obstacles.

Reverend Monsignor Ferdinand DeCneudt
August 23, 2005

Monsignor DeCneudt is retired but still active in church ministries. He resides at American House East II, a retirement community in Roseville, Michigan.

Chronology of Our Lady of Victory

1943   First baptism. Fr. Alvin Deem, a Franciscan priest, ministers among African Americans living in the vicinity of Eight Mile Road and Wyoming Avenue.

1944   City population is 4,500. Total number of sittings in church, forty-three. Archbishop Edward Mooney approves purchase of land and building of school at Wyoming Avenue and Ithaca Street in Royal Oak Township. The new site is on the fringe of a new housing project for blacks that is nearing completion. On Vigil of Pentecost, twenty converts are received into the church and make their first Holy Communion on Pentecost Sunday. Summer school at Birdhurst Recreation Center opens. Two Immaculate Heart of Mary (IHM) sisters, two lay teachers (Ida and Levina Hughes), and the pastor teach. Attendance fluctuates between 85 and 120. Use of collection envelopes begins.

1945   It becomes evident that the representatives of the Public Housing Authority were too sanguine in their promises to permit the archdiocese to acquire property in the Oakdale Gardens Housing Project. Originally estimated at $800, the price of the land rises from its appraised value of $7,500 to $8,000. This, plus the terribly excessive cost of building, makes the erection of a school impossible. City population bordering West Eight Mile Road at 7,000; will peak at 12,500. Summer school opens. Four I.H.M. sisters

and the administrator find 350 to 420 children waiting for them over the next two days. Mother Teresa
immediately sends two more sisters from Monroe to
help. The personnel send home the 100 youngest
with a mimeographed note for their parents explain-
ing the impossibility of caring for so many children.

1946   His Eminence Edward Cardinal Mooney dedicates
the new chapel erected on permanent site at 10113
West Eight Mile Road. Fr. Hubert J. Roberge takes
charge. This is the first appointment in the history of
the archdiocese of a diocesan priest to an entirely
Negro congregation.

1947   Total number of sittings in church, 226. Cardinal
Mooney confers the sacrament of confirmation for
the first time in August after the High Mass. Seven
adjacent lots on Washburn Street and two lots on
Ilene Street are purchased. Residence is taken up in
house, and lot at 20531 Washburn is acquired and
remodeled to serve as the rectory.

1948   Two lots and house at 20500 Ilene are purchased to
serve as convent at a cost of $13,275. Lot 344 is pur-
chased at a cost of $752. Four Oblate Sisters of Prov-
idence (OSP) arrive on Labor Day. They are the first
black sisters to labor in the Archdiocese of Detroit.
They stay at Holy Trinity Convent until their convent is near completion. They take up residence, and
while awaiting the day when a school would be open,
the nuns engage in catechetical instruction of children and women and do home visits.

1949   Knights and Ladies of St. Peter Claver, Santa Maria
Council #105 is organized.

1950   Four more lots are acquired to provide adequate sites
for future school. Record number of 106 baptisms
and 63 converts is the fruit of bringing the Oblate
Sisters into the apostolate.

1951   Our Lady of Victory Federal Credit Union develops, with over $200 on deposit and one loan of $35. The credit union is open for business every Friday night in the church office and on Sunday. New officers are elected at the annual meeting. A member is required to have at least $5 deposited to be entitled to vote. House and lot are acquired at 20468 Ilene to serve as home for janitor until site is needed for the future school. Increased attendance necessitates a third mass at eleven o'clock on Sundays, and a Basilian father from Assumption College comes every Sunday to assist. Charles Russell enters St. Maur Benedictine Priory, South Union, Kentucky, as a lay brother candidate.

1952   Donald Cunningham enters St. Maur Benedictine Priory as a candidate for the priesthood. Belfry is erected and set of electronic bells installed and used for the first time. First student from parish, James Oldham, enrolls in Sacred Heart Seminary.

1953   Fr. Ferdinand DeCneudt is assigned. Fr. Roberge transfers to St. Leo. The Archdiocese of Detroit grants final permission to begin plans for a five-room school. One hundred fifteen children attend Madonna, St. James, and St. Leo schools.

1954   Lot and house next to church are purchased for $7,500. House is demolished and grounds landscaped. Five-classroom school opens with a solemn dedication by Cardinal Mooney. Three Oblate Sisters of Providence and a principal, Mother Providencia, staff the school. School enrollment is eighty-six, total cost of operating the school is $85,000, and total number of registered parishioners is 285.

1955   New classroom accepting third and fourth grades opens. The principal, Mother Stella Marie, and four nuns staff the school. Reenrollment increases to 132. Holy Name Society of Men is formed.

1956   Opening of the fifth grade brings school enrollment
                to 175. Rosary Altar Society of Women forms.

1957   The last classroom and the sixth grade open. Mother
                M. Patricia is principal. Five nuns teach. School
                enrollment is 197. Property is acquired at 20500
                Washburn Street for $9,000 to provide extra space for
                sisters.

1958   Fr. DeCneudt transfers to Madonna. Seventh grade
                opens and enrollment increases to 206. Oblate Sisters
                of Providence Auxiliary Guild forms with twenty-five
                members; Catholic Youth Organization (CYO) Teen
                Club is formed with thirty members.

1959   Raymond J. Maiberger signs the financial report.
                Four-classroom addition to school completed, which
                includes additional office space for sister superior,
                clinic, and boiler facilities at cost of $65,000. Three
                nuns now living in newly purchased home at 20500
                Washburn. Concerns arise regarding a decline in
                school enrollment. Some families are unwilling to
                have children attend, are financially unable, or live
                too far away. Low-IQ or academically deficient were
                descriptions used, and a lack of space.

1960   One lay teacher and seven religious teachers staff
                school. School conducts commencement ceremony
                for the first eighth grade graduating class.

1961   His Excellency Archbishop Dearden appoints Fr.
                Walter D. Bracken administrator and assigns Fr.
                Maiberger to be pastor of St. Boniface, Detroit.
                School enrollment peaks at 242.

1962   Eight major seminarians from St. John's Seminary
                paint interior of church. The men of the parish, with
                groups from Shrine of the Little Flower and Third
                Order men from Duns Scotus, conduct a Crusade for
                Converts in honor of St. Martin's canonization. Fif-
                teen hundred pamphlets and invitations to take

instructions are distributed to non-Catholic homes. Charles Renosak, owner of Progressive Metal Co., makes and donates a ten-foot stainless-steel cross, which was later mounted to the façade of church; Lloyd Barron donates six-inch poured-aluminum letters for the façade of church.

1963   Total number of registered parishioners is 213. With a donation of $15,000 from Archbishop Dearden, parish buys the store and property west of the church. The men of the parish paint, tile, and renovate the building. It is dedicated to the Sacred Heart and all saints. The first scheduled event in the new Activity Building is the closing of Forty-Hour Dinner for the priests, with the three former pastors in attendance. The Feather Party, a Thanksgiving-season fundraiser, is held. The community is saddened by the assassination of President John F. Kennedy. Mother Patricia is replaced by Mother Charlotte. Enrollment is down to 191.

1965   Fr. Edward O'Grady is appointed administrator. Fr. Robert Monticello is appointed new weekend assistant. School enrollment is 157.

1966   Mother M. Margaretta, OSP, is assigned as principal.

1967   Total number of registered parishioners is 217. Fr. Joseph F. Ferens is assigned administrator. School enrollment is down to 143.

1970   Our Lady of Victory School closes its doors, and the students transfer to Presentation.

1975   Our Lady of Victory Church merges with Presentation Church.

1977   On February 19, Santa Maria Council #105 reorganizes under the name of Our Lady of Victory—Presentation Council/Court #189.

1982   On August 1, Our Lady of Victory officially closes its doors for the last time.

I

A Personal Perspective

Introduction

To my dismay, most folks, both in and outside of our community, have never heard of Detroit's Our Lady of Victory Church. Most of those who worshipped there are not aware of its legacy. And those who lived it are not inclined to talk about it much. But we should commend the black folks who contributed to the development of both the West Eight Mile Community and the church. They left a legacy to be proud of. They were making history; those of us who lived it became a part of it and reaped the benefits.

This book will present the facts—and some of those facts may not make for pleasant reading. I make no apologies since I had nothing to do with making the policies that shaped Our Lady of Victory and our lives; I was only a recipient. I ask that you understand that I am only the messenger. I ask this because I was totally unprepared for the hostile reaction that occurred after an early draft of the manuscript was read. I was told that the story was fascinating but that I shouldn't expect support. It was only after I received the encouragement of someone else in the diocese along with my husband's support that I continued to forge ahead. However, I did go back and take another look at the history; I decided to remove my personal opinions from the historic narrative and talk about my memories in a separate section Part I. In that way, the historical facts are not distorted. But the fact is that black people have always been on the receiving end of the negative consequences of racism. So why must we always bear the guilt for exposing it?

On a larger scale, I felt compelled to write this book because Our Lady of Victory's story is being overlooked by historians and others who write about black Catholics. For example, *The History of Black Catholics*, by Cyprian Davis, makes no specific mention of Our Lady of Victory. There are references to the Oblate Sisters of Providence, but nothing specifically tied to the church and school. *Heritage of Faith*, written by Detroit's Religious Bicentennial Task Force, completely missed Our Lady of Victory's history as well. The archdiocese has written special articles and booklets on the history of black Catholics in Detroit, but its own records list Our Lady of Victory as beginning in 1975 when it merged with Presentation. These slights and omissions must be corrected.

Living the History

Sometimes we go through life without ever realizing that history is being made around us. We encounter people who touch our lives in unexpected ways. This happens a lot in the black community. During the research phase of this project, it happened to me; I discovered the history that has surrounded me all of my life.

The credit union that was housed in the church basement is an example of history being made and overlooked. As a child, I was surprised by it but only for a moment, and then it was just another active, functioning organization in the church. In retrospect, it was rather unusual; no other church had one.

I will always treasure the wonderful memories of Our Lady of Victory (OLV) and all of the activities that it organized over the years. Sunday Masses were always packed. It was definitely the place to be if you wanted to belong, and I will be forever grateful that my parents placed me in that environment.

In the fall of 1954, my brother Ronald, my sister Joyce, and I walked into OLV to hear our first Mass. Becoming a member there brought me into contact with the Reverend Ferdinand DeCneudt, then a young priest. I learned to play the piano from Mother Anna Bates, OLV's founder. Meeting Boyce and Mary Robinson—just plain, ordinary people, who loved children—left a lasting impact on me. Mother Stella Marie was the first nun to influence me in a positive way. I met her when I started attending the brand-new school at OLV in 1955. She was a member of the historic Black Oblate Sisters of Providence based in Baltimore, Maryland.

It was through my first interview with Almeta "Dolly" Carruth-White that I learned about Richard E. Smith. After receiving a copy of his work, *Development of Our Lady of Victory and West Eight Mile*, from Ruth Green-Leonard, I embarked on a search for him. I found him through a chance encounter with Ona Carter-Harris, an OLV pioneer parishioner, at the annual St. Peter

Claver Day Mass held on September 7, 2003, in Saginaw, Michigan. Ona and
I are both members of the Knights of St. Peter Claver, Ladies Auxiliary
Courts in our respective churches. The St. Peter Claver Day Mass takes place
at a different hosting church each year, and the members turn out together in
full regalia. Ona introduced me to Marlene Ward-Talley, sister-in-law of Jean
Smith-DuPlessis and brother Emil DuPlessis. Jean led me to her brother
Richard. All of them are former children of the early pioneers of OLV, so I
was thrilled at getting the opportunity to meet and talk with them.

Choosing to go to St. Agnes high school brought Gwendolyn Keith-
Edwards into my life and gave me the opportunity to meet her wonderful parents Luther and Savella Keith. They were making their own history.

I discovered John Fleming quite by chance. I happened to call the office of
Presentation—Our Lady of Victory Church, and Sr. Mary Elise answered the
phone. When I told her who I was, she said, with excitement in her voice,
"There is someone I want you to meet!" Now, I had not said anything to her
about my project, but something or someone led her to tell me about John. I
went to see him, and the rest is history, so to speak. We shared some wonderful memories. He also worked with Keith on community projects.

When I met with him, he was working on an exhibit of the Oblate Sisters
of Providence to be put on display at St. Aloysius Church during Black History Month in February 2003. He does this every year. He provided materials,
such as *The Oblate News and Views,* that carried articles about OLV, complete
with pictures. I had not seen those periodicals in many years.

John is a walking history of the black experience in the Catholic Church.
He lives in Detroit and is a member of St. Aloysius Parish in downtown
Detroit.

I never would have known the history behind these individuals if I had not
made the decision to write this book. I would not have known Richard Smith
or the research he did about the development of historic black Royal Oak
Township and Our Lady of Victory Mission Church. I never knew about any
of this growing up, and, well, you get the picture. We just lived by the foundation the pioneers laid out for us. How could we know, if no one shared this
with us? We couldn't! And so, we just coasted through life, unaware of the
legacy we had been given. Writing this book gives new meaning and understanding to my life and makes me proud to be a part of this black history.

†

My parents are Curtis and Joyce Giles. I am the second born of eight children—Ronald Powell, Joyce Marie, Rudolph James, twins Milton Dewey and Melvin Dwight, Constance Winifred, and Teresa Avaline. Father, who migrated from Mississippi seeking a job in Detroit, was a manager at Ford Motor Co. Mother was born in Depew, Oklahoma, and raised in California after both her parents and her only brother, Bill, died. She was a homemaker, a poet, a storyteller, and a great speaker. My parents met in California through mutual friends. They married, and my dad arranged for Mother to stay with relatives in Royal Oak Township until I was born. He was on active duty in the navy, stationed in Guam during World War II. Mother left California and arrived by train at the Michigan Central Depot in Detroit with my brother Ronald, who was a toddler at the time.

Mother told me that while she was traveling, she became ill and uncomfortable with her pregnancy, so Ronald asked the attendant, "Please bring my mother some water; she's not feeling good." (Remember, he was not quite two years old). I knew that my brother was wonderful, but hearing that story from Mother made him seem even more awesome. I always looked up to him, and so did all our friends.

When we came of school age, my brother, sister, and I started attending George Washington Carver Elementary School. While living in Royal Oak Township, we were not exposed to door-to-door evangelization. It's interesting how my mother found out about the church.

For some time, she had noticed a young boy walking, very early in the morning, past our two-story project housing unit at 10729 Hinsdale Court. He wore blue pants, a white shirt, and a tie. She was so impressed with his appearance that she just had to find out where he was going. She stopped him one morning and asked. He told her that he was attending the new school affiliated with Our Lady of Victory Church. My parents immediately sought out this church and started taking instructions, because they wanted us enrolled in the school. Mother was doing just what the other parents were doing—looking for a good education for her children. The boy's name was Frank Cryer, and we became classmates. Walking to school dressed in a uniform was a kind of evangelization, because it sure made an impression on our mother. As soon as the school doors opened, we were right there. Around this time, my whole family started attending OLV and preparing to become baptized Catholics.

With the help of our godmother, Martha Palms-Williams, my severely retarded brother, Rudolph James, was baptized a year before the rest of the family and placed in an institution in Lapeer, Michigan. When they took him away, he turned around and reached out his hands for Mother. It was so amazing that he knew that he was leaving her. He knew who she was in spite of his handicap. It was also a sad thing to see, and I cried so hard for him and my mother that day. Yet I was relieved. It had been very stressful on the family. Because he was so handicapped, we could not lead a normal family life. We never saw him again. I do not recall him getting baptized before the rest of the family, but there it was in the records. I can certainly see the urgency of it, looking back. We got help for him only after coming to Our Lady of Victory and meeting those wonderful, Christian people.

Years later, Mother received a letter from the State of Michigan informing her that Rudy had been dropped during the birthing process, and that was the cause of his retardation. Apparently, there had been an investigation. Mother could have filed a lawsuit, but her faith in God would not allow it. The faith came from her association with Our Lady of Victory. This church profoundly influenced her, and it helped her through this stressful period in our lives. As I sit here at my computer writing about this incident, I am emotionally distraught. It still hurts after all these years, and I still feel the guilt of leaving him in that institution, even though I had nothing to do with any of it.

Unfortunately, my father was not baptized, and eventually my parents separated. We experienced some financial hardships, and that was when the kindness of the parish family became so important to our mother and to our very existence.

My mother, a politician in her own right, found a way to keep us in Catholic schools. Our godmother came through for us and paid our tuition every year until each of us graduated from high school. We are talking about seven children who received her help. She was wealthy and took her role as godmother seriously. Not many do what she did, and I love her for it, because I thoroughly enjoyed going to Our Lady of Victory Catholic School. She was a saint and a true godmother. It took years for me to realize the significance of her generosity. But once I came to the realization of what she had done, I sent her a bouquet of roses while she could still smell them along with a thank-you note.

She died not too long after that, around 1988. I took a call from Madeline Fortier, an early pioneer, who informed us of Martha's death. I was employed at the *Detroit Free Press* at the time and was having such a hellish time with the Joint Operating Agreement (J.O.A.) turmoil going on there that I missed the funeral. My mother didn't go, either, because she had no way to get there. I assumed that Mother would be taken to the funeral by other church members after I put the word out about Martha's death. I know now that it was the wrong assumption on my part, and I regret not making personal arrangements for Mother to get there. We were very fortunate to have Martha in our lives, and that is what coming to Our Lady of Victory meant for us.

There was always a problem with the boiler in the new school, so we sat in the classroom many days with our coats on. It broke down too often and got very cold. Some days we were sent home. I remember Mother being very pregnant and walking through six inches of snow just to bring our lunches to school so that we wouldn't go hungry. I was about nine or ten years old, and that was when I realized how much she really loved us. She looked very uncomfortable and should not have been walking in that kind of weather, but she did, and then she had to turn around and walk all the way back home. That day I was deeply touched by my mother's gesture of love and very worried for her safety. I prayed that she would not fall down going home. Her faith in her church and her love for us had made a lasting impression on me.

My mother, in my mind, should have been more than just a homemaker. She was certainly gifted, and, most of all, she talked to us and listened to our problems. Many times when we had to write an essay or story, she helped us with our homework assignments. I always got As on my papers.

I recall Mother helping me with a speech we students had to write for Fr. DeCneudt's departure. Mother Patricia was so impressed with what I had written that the other children didn't get a chance to read theirs. She didn't know that Mother had a hand in it. I also remember being very sad that Fr. DeCneudt was leaving and wondering what was going to happen to us.

✝

William Dewey Burkes and Leslie Louise Allen were my grandparents. He was a professor and a minister, and she was a schoolteacher. They died when Mother was very young and left her and her brother Bill orphaned. Uncle Bill drowned trying to save someone's life, and Mother was all alone in the world.

She lost an advantage when they passed away too soon. Aunt Beatrice Strass-
ner removed her from a school she was attending in Oklahoma and took her
back to California to live with relatives. None of them were as caring as a
mother would be. She said that her Aunt Bea just walked into the classroom
and took her away. She never got the chance to say good-bye to Mr. and Mrs.
Davis, her guardians. In 1945, on her way to Detroit, she stopped to see them
one last time before heading to her new life in Royal Oak Township. I felt so
sorry for my mother when she told that story. She was a very brave person. She
wanted to be the mother to us that she never had, and she was extraordinary at
it. She could have given us away. Thank God she didn't.

My mother could recite a Bible verse and have the audience on its feet in a
standing ovation. I witnessed this, and that is when I realized the gift my
mother possessed. Many of my friends told her how she had influenced them
and how much they admired her strength. I was happy that my friends
thought well of her. Her peers described her as a "woman of great faith." I am
still trying to emulate her faith and strong character.

I remember when a dear friend of mine, Gwenda McDonald, came up
from Dallas, Texas, for a visit and discovered that my mother had a collection
of poems published. She was so excited because, even though we had known
one another for years, she didn't know that my mother wrote poetry. I never
thought to tell her. Because of her enthusiasm, I also got excited that day. A
sister-in-law, Lorraine, was surprised, as well, when she learned of Mother's
poems and talked to her from time to time about her works. My son, Clyde,
should have been a journalist, because he writes extremely well. He can express
his ideas in a way that can be profound and thought-provoking.

I met Gwendolyn Keith-Edwards as a freshman in high school. She is the
daughter of Luther C. Keith, a prominent black Catholic who, while not a
member of Our Lady of Victory, has forged a place in its history. I was
amazed to learn this and that he was a major player in the city of Detroit's
political arena. I met him through Gwen at their family home in Detroit.

He was appointed by the Knights of St. Peter Claver National Council to
organize the Detroit branch. Our Lady of Victory was to be the designated
headquarters. As I continued my research, it became evident that the Claver
organization left a lasting impact on the black church in Detroit. Many of the
pioneers remain active in the organization today, scattered throughout the
Northern District, which is comprised of nineteen states in the Midwest, East
Coast, and New England areas.

Gwen and I became lifelong friends without my ever knowing of her father's contributions to the city of Detroit and Our Lady of Victory. It is not that she was trying to keep it from me, or anyone for that matter, but her brother Luther explains it this way. "We just took our father's contributions for granted, not realizing he was making history." Their parents were people who entertained religious and political leaders in their home.

This is exactly what happened in my own family with our mother. We children took her gifts for granted, not realizing until it was pointed out by friends what a talented individual she was. This goes back to what I said initially, that we do not know our history, and we don't always know when we are living it until someone writes about it.

Gwen and I just naturally gravitated to one another when I started my freshman year at St. Agnes High School (renamed Martyrs of the Uganda and now closed). I was so shy, and she made me feel welcome that very first day. She was so nice, and we became instant friends. I don't know why I chose this school; I didn't do any research, and I didn't discuss it with any teacher or my friends. I chose it from several options that were presented to me. When I found out it was an all girls school, I asked my mother if I could go to Mumford High School, a public school in Detroit. She said, "No!" So fate brought me to St. Agnes and into the lives of the Keith family. I am a firm believer that we are where we are supposed to be at any given time in this life.

Gwen and her family were longtime members of St. Agnes Church and School, which included a combined grade school and high school. We managed to stay in touch over the years. I even went to see her and her husband Cleve at their home in Fairfax Station, Virginia, in 1993. We shared some wonderful high school memories. How small this world is that her father indirectly affected my life in a positive way. It was truly amazing to discover that he had a part in my church's beginnings. When Gwen introduced me to her mother, Savella Keith, for the first time, her mother made me feel as if we were old friends. I always felt special around her each time I came to visit, because she was so kind to me. Not many people have that rare gift of making you feel good about yourself.

I discovered that Fr. Ferdinand DeCneudt, third pastor of Our Lady of Victory, worked with Luther Keith on various community projects in the fifties. Fr. DeCneudt was saying Mass when we walked into the church that September morning. I thought Our Lady of Victory was the most beautiful church I had ever seen, and father was beautiful, too. The church décor was so tasteful, and just being there was soothing to the senses. Fr. DeCneudt (he was elevated to monsignor in later years) told me that the decorating credit goes to the previous priest, Fr. Hubert Roberge, who was great at interior design. Fr. DeCneudt baptized my family and many other families during his tenure. He was the only pastor I really knew, so it was a real shocker to learn years later that he was just an administrator. A pastor is permanently installed in a church. An administrator is assigned on a temporary basis. We didn't know the difference at the time, but it would deeply affect the survival of OLV in the coming years.

Another thing that made a profound impression on me was discovering, when I got to St. Agnes, that the pastor, Rev. Frank J. McQuillan, had been there well over two decades. It was like a culture shock coming from Our Lady of Victory. Fr. DeCneudt was gone before I graduated. I knew him as a child, and so, quite naturally, he was stamped in my memory even though he was there for just a short while. Everybody had grown fond of him. Some of the members kept a lasting relationship with him the same as those who kept up with Fr. Alvin Deem. I was fortunate to find the monsignor in recent years. I don't remember much about the priests that came later—there were just too many of them.

✝

When you attend a parochial school, you usually get a chance to go on field trips that offer examples of living a good Christian life. Our school went to see *The Ten Commandments* at one of several theaters in downtown Detroit. If my memory serves me correctly, it was at the United Artist, which was a premiere theatre in the fifties. We were so excited about going to the movie, because some of us didn't get the chance to go very often. As soon as we stepped off the bus, I experienced another culture shock. We were one group of black children among a sea of white children coming from all parts of the city and suburbs. I thought there were black Catholics everywhere, but this experience soon dispelled any misconceptions I ever had about race. I had truly led a sheltered life; all I ever saw was black people in my church and in my community. I became very aware of the differences between them and us, and it was unsettling to me. I was out of my comfort zone for the first time in my life. I experienced this same phenomenon during my high school years, and it was definitely a learning experience.

Amazingly, this was never talked about at OLV, and even though we had diversity at St. Agnes, it wasn't discussed there either, nor was it discussed at home. We learned the lessons about race disparity in silence and in an unconscious state of mind.

I was learning the lessons when I saw a white garbage man driving his truck through our black neighborhood while the black garbage man with him was doing all the hard work by himself. He was very dirty and had a white substance all over his body; kind of like soot, a film that came from picking up trash cans that burned garbage at the time. I was amazed at seeing him mistreated this way. Some of the white people I did meet were very nice—like the milkman, the Good Humor ice-cream man, and our pastor. The insurance man and the numbers man (responsible for illegal payouts when a number hit for a win just like the legal lottery) were black, and there were some black-owned and black-run businesses in the neighborhood. The township had Cunningham's Drug Store, A&P, a jewelry store, the five-and ten-cent store (much like the dollar stores that have popped up all over the region), a shoe store, a men's clothing store, and Dr. Richard Snowden's office—the only black dentist in the township. We also had a movie house called the Duke Theatre. My brother Ronald used to wind up staying there all night whenever he ran away from home, which was often. But at least he was safe.

My mother drilled it into us that we were just as good as anyone, which took the sting out of anything negative that we saw in our young lives. Her teachings gave us the confidence to step out into the world. And while we had less negative baggage to handle in our later lives, being naïve did prove to be a slight handicap.

I recall seeing a significant number of altar boys after we arrived at OLV. I was fascinated with what they were doing at the altar. They rang a bell during the consecration of the bread and wine. They lit the candles before Mass and snuffed them out when Mass ended. They placed linens on the altar before Mass and then removed them when Mass ended. They assisted the priest as needed during the service. All of this looked so dramatic and impressive and sacred to me. There were so many teens and young boys serving on a rotating basis. OLV had all the ingredients of a thriving, growing Catholic community with the real possibility of nurturing future priests.

Vondie Curtis Hall was one of the altar boys. His name was so unusual that it unconsciously stuck with me; and when I saw him listed on a TV show, I knew it was the boy from Our Lady of Victory School. He appeared in the popular movie *Coming to America* and has other works to his credit. He attended our class reunion in 2002. I didn't know him personally and would not have been able to pick him out in a crowd, but I remembered that name. He had a sister and a brother, and they always came to church together, well dressed, and sat in the front row. Everyone always had a particular seat that they claimed every Sunday, so it often happened that you were known by where you chose to sit—not necessarily by your name.

I can recall walking to church from the township early in the morning and hearing those church bells and thinking how beautiful they sounded. And it was awesome that they could be heard from such a distance. I loved those chimes that beckoned us to Mass on weekdays and Sunday mornings. My sister Connie loved hearing them, as well. I remember the altar boys' duties included the task of pulling the ropes to start the chimes. It was extremely loud up close. I was thinking—those boys had to get up awfully early to ring those bells and serve at Mass. That required lots of discipline. I admired them for being so responsible at such a young age, because I knew I could barely get out of bed each morning. At a time when many teenagers had no direction, the teens and young men who served as altar boys at OLV seemed to have it together, just serving God. I could tell that they were going places in life. I guess you can tell what an impression those altar boys made on me. I thought about them often in my life. I admired them so much.

✝

When my family came to the church, the Oblate Sisters of Providence were a big influence in our lives and a big hit for the parish. Our teacher, Mother Stella Marie, was such an interesting person, and I looked forward to attending class every day just to see her. Having started out at George Washington Carver Elementary in Royal Oak Township, I thought this new faith my parents had found was quite an experience, to say the least. Especially seeing the nuns wear those garments called habits. I could not take my eyes off them, because we had never seen anything like it. I loved going to school, and we got a superior education. Later in life, while taking some courses at Wayne County Community College—which I thoroughly enjoyed—students noticed how quick I was in class. They often asked, "Where did you go to school?" I attribute it to those early years of training at OLV. The nuns were stern disciplinarians, and they taught us how to respect people of authority. We didn't know anything about the race problem in our little corner of the world. The only thing we knew was what our parents and those nuns taught us.

What can I say about Mother Stella Marie except that she was the first nun that I ever laid eyes on, and I thought she was beautiful. She was gentle and stern at the same time, which could give you mixed signals. She was tall and regal in her veil and garment. She commanded authority. I had her for the fourth and fifth grades. We made our first Holy Communion and confirmation under her guidance. We girls were enrolled in the Junior Sodality of OLV, and once a month we turned out in those powder blue capes and floppy tams at High Mass. High Masses were always formal and had a full choir while the Low Mass did not have a choir.

I remember being transfixed by the stories that Mother Stella Marie told. She had a quick wit and was always telling stories that mesmerized us. We would sit spellbound, hanging on every word in anticipation of what was coming next. She and Mother Patricia, who was the next mother superior, knew how to get our attention and stretch our imaginations. They always laced the stories with some profound truth that was to help us throughout our lives. I looked forward to hearing those stories.

I can recall countless times when we children got sick or fainted during the 8:00 AM Mass because we were not used to going without breakfast, and our stomachs let us know it. In those days, church law stated that you could not have breakfast before receiving communion; so when Mass was over, we marched in line to school and ate our breakfast in the classroom. There was no lunchroom.

I remember getting sick at a funeral Mass once and almost fainting. Mother Stella Marie took my sister Joyce and me over to the convent for breakfast when she discovered that we had not eaten that morning. On this one rare occasion that we were allowed to enter the convent, I saw bright yellow walls in the kitchen and marveled at how clean and shiny the floors were. I never saw a room so spotless in my life. It was breathtaking to see, and I was in awe. Those nuns kept that convent sparkling clean. Msgr. DeCneudt told me that during the planning stage, the diocese thought that the nuns should have a bigger convent. They didn't want it. They were satisfied with what they had.

After that fainting spell, Mother Stella Marie made sure that Joyce and I got milk and baked goods every day. She paid special attention to us that I didn't really welcome but understood. When Mother Patricia arrived, she also gave us free milk and baked goods. I didn't feel comfortable being treated like a charity case. It was a constant reminder that my father was absent from the home. It was something people kept quiet about and went on with life. I pretended that none of this was happening, and that was how I coped with it.

Mother Stella Marie taught poetry and music in the spare room. Some of the poems were truly profound. I must quote one that stayed with me over the years:

> I have only just one minute.
> Only sixty seconds in it.
> Forced upon me, can't refuse it.
> Didn't seek it, didn't choose it.
> But it's up to me to use it.
> I must suffer if I lose it.
> Give account if I abuse it.
> Just a tiny little minute,
> But eternity is in it.

I have often found myself repeating this poem. It probably explains why I do not like to waste time doing nonproductive things. I never gave it much thought until now. It just shows you the effect that someone can have on your life. And Mother Stella Marie definitely had a positive effect on mine. I never saw her again after she left OLV, but I will never forget her.

Mother Patricia taught us in the sixth, seventh, and eighth grades. She was a plain-looking, soft-spoken, no-nonsense kind of person. She had certain sayings that her students heard often. One of her favorites was, "Get an education, or you will be digging ditches for the rest of your life." Mother Patricia also would say, "I make a dime in the morning and a dime in the afternoon." We were mortified to hear that she made very little money. I never forgot this, because when you are a child, you are so trusting and gullible, and she was dead serious when she said it. A couple of her other sayings were: "Hell is paved with good intentions" and "You will find yourself walking on tissue paper over hell." I don't quite remember it word for word, just the part about the tissue paper and hell. She would make remarks that kept us thinking on our feet. That's how clever she was. She was the mother superior of the first class to graduate from OLV School in June of 1960.

Before those nuns, we never knew anything about a religious order. They were the first nuns most of us ever met, and knowing them left an indelible impression on all of us. They were making history as the only black nuns in the diocese, and all that history surrounded us.

I saw Mother Patricia ten or twelve years ago, and I was struck by how tiny she was. She, too, has passed on.

OLV School ceased to exist by 1970. I met Sister Sharon Young when she taught my son Clyde at the merged Presentation—Our Lady of Victory School. I never knew her from OLV, although she and her family were active members. I did not know that she was a part of OLV's history until my interview with Dolly. Sr. Sharon has become very close to me and especially to Clyde over the years.

My encounter with the Home Visitors of Mary (H.V.M.) came in the person of Sister Barbara Dakoske when she was assigned to the merged Presentation and Our Lady of Victory. Sr. Barbara entered H.V.M. in 1957 and served at Presentation—Our Lady of Victory in the early 1990s. She visited my home and helped my mother make her last journey through this life in August 1991.

I knew Sister Mary Schutz was a nun but had no knowledge of the history of the Home Visitors of Mary and their ties to OLV through her, but her name came up in documents from early members and church files. And so being the curious person that I am, I decided to find out who Sr. Mary was. The result is a section in Part II about her contributions to OLV's history.

✝

The parish was so full, and I was glad just to be a part of it, because it was exciting to belong—like a real family with the same things in common. And it didn't hurt that there were quite a few cute boys, too. I have never seen anything like it since—ever! And speaking of family, coming into the church is how I met the Boyce and Mary Robinson family. They were angels who were a positive influence on my early years. Their home was like an open house, and my brother, sister, and I practically lived over there and ate Sunday dinners there many times. Boyce Sr. (now deceased), Mary, and their children were like a second family, and it was a real treat being around them. It seemed as if every child in the neighborhood went through the Robinsons' doors at one time or another. They had their own children and everybody else's. It was like the United Nations, because there were foreign children that passed through their doors, as well. We spent half of our childhood there. I will never forget how kind they were.

I used to stop by the home of Ruth Rosa Green-Leonard on the way to school to walk with her daughter Carol. I remember the oldest daughter,

Angela, and how gorgeous and sophisticated she was, and how I wanted to be just like her when I grew up. Irma was the third daughter, and Arthur "Skip" III was the last child and only son. I remember their grandmother, Mary, who lived over one hundred years. She was a very petite woman. Ruth's father, Antonio Rosa, seemed to me to be very devoted to Mary. I always saw the two of them together when I visited. Even as a child, I could tell that they had something special. I remember him having a head full of white straight hair and a distinct white mustache. Ruth took care of her mother until the day her mother died.

Washington Leonard married Ruth after both their spouses passed on, and that is how she became a Leonard. The first time I laid eyes on Washington was when he brought a big turkey and a basket of food to our home for Thanksgiving, courtesy of St. Vincent de Paul. That was my introduction to those wonderful and kind people of OLV. After my parents separated, we had some difficult times. Washington was one of the principal persons responsible for providing assistance to those in need through the society. Washington had such a great sense of humor—he could tell a good joke. I remember his visits to see my mother when she became gravely ill. His sense of humor helped us through this difficult time. I will never forget his kindness to my family both at that time and during the early years. His kindness and goodness made a positive impact on my life. He was a true Christian in every sense of the word, a great role model who lived his faith until his death. It seemed like every priest that was assigned to Our Lady of Victory and Presentation attended Washington's funeral. That is the legacy of Washington Leonard. I am glad that I had the chance to know him. Because of the example he set, today I give to St. Vincent De Paul, the church, the Goodfellows, and other charities.

✝

The day we made our first Holy Communion, about 90 percent of the school was Catholic, and more were converting. We had to wear white dresses and a long, hanging veil over our heads, white slippers, and white dressy socks. I could not wait to receive the host—the body of Christ—for the first time, and that is what the ceremony was all about. I remember the delicious food, the beautiful decorations in the church hall, and what a wonderful experience it all was. Those wonderful women in the church prepared a delicious breakfast of pancakes, soft scrambled eggs, sausage, bacon, and toast with hot cocoa, real white tablecloths, silverware, and beautiful dishes. It was awesome being the center of so much attention.

Confirmation usually took place around the age of twelve, and you had to have a sponsor. Mother Robinson, as she was affectionately called, was my sponsor, and over the years, we have remained very close. Getting confirmed made you a complete Christian. You were called "soldiers of Christ," and you had to choose a second name. I chose Lucy as my second name. At the confirmation ceremony, I was waiting for the "tongues of fire" to appear out of the ceiling. "Tongues of fire" was an expression that denoted a cleansing of the spirit. I took it literally, because of the way the priest preached about it in his sermons. His "fire and brimstone" style of preaching would have made you believe anything. I was so disappointed when those flames didn't show up.

I remember learning about the infamous "wall" while a student at OLV. Some of my classmates pointed it out. I was stunned that it was built to separate the races. By the time we came to the church, it was just a reminder of that sad period. I did not believe it for a long time, because I could not imagine that anything this far-fetched could have actually happened. It is still there, a thick, gray concrete slab in the alley between Birwood and Mendota Streets.

✝

Somehow, we were sheltered from blatant racism. Although we saw things that were questionable, we were just too young to understand it. As we grew older, it was so subtle that we didn't know what was really going on until it hit us in the face. Growing up in an all-black neighborhood does that to you. Black people had a way of shutting out the reality of what was happening to them. My parents never discussed the problems of racism. While my father suffered outright discrimination in his life, my mother grew up in an integrated environment out in California, so she had an idealistic view of the world. She even experienced interracial dating, learning about other cultures. My father, on the other hand, was an alcoholic. He severed his ties with family back in Mississippi, so we never knew our grandparents, aunts, and uncles on his side. And because Mother was an orphan, we never knew our grandparents on her side. Mother never accepted racism. It was someone else's problem. Both my parents had their way of coping.

In 1954, OLV was only taking children up to the second grade, and so Joyce started second grade there, and to my surprise, my brother Ronald started fourth grade, and I started third grade at Madonna and St. Paul (now called Church of the Madonna Parish) on Oakman Boulevard. We were never told that we would be repeating a grade. Neither one of us had ever failed any of our subjects while attending Carver School. We boarded the chartered bus waiting in front of the church each morning after Mass and we were bused across town to our classes. Apparently, Madonna was the only Catholic school that was accepting a bus load of black children.

I remember reading before I started kindergarten, around three or four years of age. I did not know that there was something extraordinary in being able to do that, yet I was put back a grade in order to attend Madonna school. My brother was even smarter. It was wrong to be judged by the color of your skin and the school you came from just because it did not meet the establishment's so-called standards. That was an insult to the educated teachers who taught us.

With so many priest assigned to our church, there should be no surprise that I found questionable reasons for low attendance at OLV School in the archives. I fully recovered from the shock of seeing in writing that OLV students had low IQs. Can you imagine what must have been said when all of us landed at Madonna? I am sure the establishment must have been quite distressed to see so many black youngsters descending on their school all at once. Putting us back a grade may have been a way to discourage this attendance or keep the numbers down.

I guess our parents were so desperate for us to get a good education that they were willing to sacrifice us to get it. They never asked us how we felt about it. I was so ashamed and humiliated by the experience that I wouldn't talk about it for years. As I started writing this book, I knew I had to come to terms with my feelings, because I get butterflies in my stomach to this day just thinking about what we went through. I discovered, however, that we were not the only ones to experience this humiliation.

Third- and fourth-grades were added to OLV the following year, and I began attending there. Madonna stopped taking the children of OLV, and Ronald went to Our Lady of Sorrows in Detroit. The chartered bus was eliminated. Anyway, I was not privy to enough inside information to question why these things happened. Looking back, it all seems rather sad that my brother and other students had to go to a Catholic school so far from home at such a young age. I never really thought much about how he got there every day.

Going to Madonna afforded us a chance to ride a chartered bus. After that changed, families were on their own getting their children to a Catholic school in the city of Detroit.

I suppose we had it better than the children before us, because Dolly said that they had to go to Sacred Heart, which is near Gratiot Avenue and the eastern market and had to catch several buses to get there. Some of the children living on the east side of Wyoming in Royal Oak Township were fortunate to go to St. James on Nine Mile Road. Public and private schools did not accept the children living on the west side of Wyoming in the same township. The high school children were bused to Northern High in Detroit before bussing became a coined phrase and a controversial issue. When the bussing ended, the Royal Oak Township parents had to get a court order to force Oak Park Schools to accept their children.

We resided on the west side of Wyoming, and our mother did not want us to be a part of that kind of rejection, so she took us out of the public school system. Quite a few residents of the West Eight Mile Community took great pains to get their children into good schools. It was very hard back then, so people cherished a good education. Being very young had its good points … you were not aware of the problems that you may have gone through, because they were just too profound and too complex to comprehend. Youth has its innocence and its protection.

I missed my brother very much when we had to go to separate schools. When we were in public school, he had always looked out for us. Now we were on our own. He started going to Our Lady of Sorrows on Meldrum in Detroit, and I suppose he got with other children to get there. I remember it being very popular for many of the teenagers to attend St. Leo High School, and I wondered why. I found my answer in the OLV archives. Fr. Hubert Roberge was transferred to St. Leo. It seems obvious now that the parents of OLV followed him there. You see black children were not welcome at many white parochial schools at that time. That has not changed very much over the years, which is why saving OLV should have been a top priority.

†

I have heard repeatedly that you cannot force people to come into the Catholic Church, but it worked for OLV because people wanted to be there. Msgr. DeCneudt said, "Parents had to study the faith if they wanted their children to attend the school. They did not necessarily have to become Catholic, but many of them did."

The mixing of Catholic and non-Catholic children in inner city schools left black Catholic parents in a dilemma: how to give their children the Catholic education they remembered as children. I had Catholic friends who took their children out of Presentation School and put them somewhere else, trying to give them an education that they felt the children were lacking. I had non-Catholic friends who put their children in Presentation looking for the same thing. This has been going on for years. So consequently, the parish members did not wholeheartedly support the school, and this created the necessity to take in more non-Catholic children. Classrooms had to be filled somehow to make them sustainable.

When I enrolled Clyde at Presentation, I thought he was going to have the same wonderful experience I received. But in the eighties, things had changed and not for the better, I might add. How out of touch I was, having been away from church for a few years.

There were children of mixed faith attending when Clyde arrived. He was taught by a brother, a nun, and lay teachers, so I was somewhat surprised that he had to take religious education outside of class time, just like the public school children had to do. I was also surprised that the parishioners did not seem to have a stake in the school anymore. I realized how much I missed while away and how crucial that information could be to the decisions I made about how best to educate my child.

In recent years, Clyde told me that he had no good memories attending Presentation—OLV School. I was very surprised and unprepared to hear this and sad as well, because I tried so hard to give him a good basic education. I remember getting a call at work from Mother, who was caring for him, telling me to come home, because she was concerned about him. I got home as fast as I could. We went into the bedroom, and he started crying, pouring his little heart out about how the kids didn't want to include him in basketball. He was in the fourth grade, and I had just put him in the school, so he was the new kid on the block. My heart just broke seeing him so distraught. While this kind of thing goes on, it just never happened to my son, who was so outgoing and personable for his age and who generally had no trouble making friends. He was small for his age, and so he did have a few challenges to overcome, but he was gutsy and could stand up to the best of them. I comforted him, gave him lots of hugs and some advice, and we did get through this crisis.

The point of this story is to stress that a black parent should try to make sure that there is a good fit with their children and the school they are attending. In my case, it would have meant pulling my child out of Presentation—OLV Catholic School. I know that some of my peers had done this. A similar scene probably played out more frequently than one may think, which may have contributed to the exodus of black Catholic children out of changing Catholic schools in the city of Detroit.

I sent Clyde to the University of Detroit High School. At thirteen, he was among the youngest and smallest children there. However, that did not stop him from trying out for football. The coach refused to let him play, because he was too small, and the possibility of injury was real. Clyde once told the coach, "We would have won if you had let me play." The coach was astounded at his confidence and told me about it at a parent-teacher conference. The coach always referred to him as "that little guy." That's the impression Clyde would leave on people. He never ceases to amaze me, and I'm his mother. He was an amazing youngster, so much like my brother in many ways.

Clyde transferred out of the U of D High in his sophomore year and graduated from Oak Park High School in 1986. I did succeed in providing a basic education for him, but only because I was an involved parent. But at what cost? If I had it to do all over again, I would make sure that the school my child attends is a good fit in every way. Because we had moved around a little, I was not sure if he had even gotten the basics in elementary school, so I gave him a test to find out if he had missed anything by asking a simple question. "Which fraction is bigger, one-third or one-fourth?" He said, "one-third" and I said, "*Yes!* You got it!" That is what it is all about, and what it has always been about for black parents—paying some kind of price to get that education, even unintentionally sacrificing our own children.

✝

I graduated from OLV in June of 1960. Fr. Roberge attended and took a photo of the first graduates on the church grounds. I had no idea who he was and wondered over the years why he was in the class photo. I don't know if we were ever told about him, but I never knew much except what I had heard over the years about his legacy. I certainly didn't know him at our ceremony. Later, I found his photo in the archives and compared it with our graduation picture. Then his presence at our graduation made sense.

I realized even as a child that this event was a historic moment, and I did wonder why Fr. DeCneudt was not there, sharing in our milestone. Maybe he was overlooked. Nevertheless, for me there was a void left by him not being there that day.

As much as I hated history in school, I always felt a fondness for it but not on a conscious level. In reality, I loved it, only I didn't know it. It would take years for me to discover this. Confusing, isn't it? That's because the history I was learning about was conflicted and contradictory, and there was nothing to pique my interest.

On June 23, 1965, Fr. Edward O'Grady was appointed the administrator of Our Lady of Victory. I was feeling detached from the church, and my attendance became sporadic. When you are young and inexperienced, you are already going through a confused state of mind, and seeing your church in such turmoil does not help. It felt like everything around me was changing for the worse, and that was very unsettling.

You see, I lost my brother, Lance Corporal Ronald L. Powell, to the Vietnam War in August 1965. There was an explosion over the Hong Kong River, and all seventy-five men aboard the plane he was on perished. He was in the marines, and he received a military funeral at OLV and a twenty-one-gun salute at Holy Sepulchre Cemetery. An article about him ran in the *Detroit News*. I was devastated, and as they played "Taps," my eyes flooded with tears. I didn't even know the priest who said the funeral Mass. I learned during the research that it was Fr. Edward O'Grady.

The parish family rallied around us. We did not have to do anything. They brought over food and took care of our mother. Two marines stood at attention at our home and at Halls Funeral Home, guarding his casket. There was no body—only a dog tag identifying his remains. This revelation so traumatized me that I started sleepwalking and turning on the lights in our bedroom. I also developed insomnia. Joyce told me that I got out of our bunk bed (I slept on top), turned on the light, and then got back into bed. I found it hard to believe, but stress will do a lot of things to the body.

From 1967 to 1970, Fr. Joseph Ferens, another priest I had no memories of, was assigned to the parish. In 1968, I was engaged to be married. My fiancé and I arrive for a meeting with this new priest, and he failed to keep the appointment! I was mortified that we were stood up on one of the most important days of my life.

I suppose he may have had a problem with the fact that I was pregnant. Because of my condition, Mother was frantic and insisted that I go and see him. This was my very first meeting with Fr. Ferens, and I was reluctant about going. Once we finally did meet, he asked me, "What are your future plans?" We had just gotten engaged, and so I said, "To get married and move in with his parents until we are able to afford a place of our own." Evidently he took issue with those plans, because he muttered an unflattering remark, which was racially biased, but I cannot recall it. I do remember getting up and leaving.

Ultimately, a minister in my fiancé's faith married us. I am not trying to paint what happened in a negative light. I am telling it from the perspective of how I was personally affected by an administrator who didn't know me at all, and I didn't know him. Prior to researching this, I couldn't recall his name and didn't remember what he looked like.

I do know that my church lost something, and we were never able to get it back. People were leaving. Most of my classmates were gone. The church of my memories, that shaped me as a child, was dying a slow death. I was grieving for a long time, devastated by the death of my brother and the slow death of my church. It was a very bad time for me.

After getting married, I dropped out of the church altogether. At that time, you were excommunicated if you married outside the faith. Eventually, I came back divorced and with a small child. The Catholic Church was all I knew. My life was a mess for a while, because I had lost my direction and was disillusioned by what I thought was a Christian, God-fearing, faith-filled church. Unfortunately, we held priests to a higher standard, and we set ourselves up for a letdown.

My life was a lesson in contradictions. I was told that I had to get an annulment before I could remarry. Why would you annul a marriage that had produced a child? I disagreed with that advice. I had to find a single man who had no marriage in his history before I could be married in the Catholic Church. How many single, black, Catholic men can you find in the city of Detroit? What were they thinking when they gave me this advice? Although I did manage to meet a number of single men, not all of them were marriage material, and they certainly were not Catholic.

Most of my Catholic girlfriends didn't fare much better. The problem with all of these rules was that they did not apply very well to the black community. We had a whole set of social problems and issues that the white establishment was not prepared to deal with or even acknowledge. I say this because if they had kept our church open and helped it to flourish, maybe I would have had a choice of marrying a Catholic and would not have had these issues to deal with. If I had followed their rules, I would have had to remain single. We have enough single parents in the black community already. I chose to stay away longer until the rules changed. Eventually they did. There was a big ceremony at Blessed Sacrament Cathedral forgiving all the fallen Catholics in one swoop. I did not attend the ceremony. I was questioning everything at that time.

Langston (my present husband of twenty-four years) and I eventually renewed our vows at Presentation—OLV Church. Fr. Ed Scheurmann—a priest who was there only for the year 2000—performed the ceremony. We went through Fr. Kenneth Stewart who was the presiding priest, to file the proper papers. By the time the papers were approved, the archdiocese mistakenly sent them to Fr. Stewart in Chicago where he had transferred during the process. Even the archdiocese has a hard time keeping up with the revolving door of priests in and out of the parish. Otherwise they would have known that Fr. Stewart was transferred from the parish and the paperwork should not have gone to Chicago. Fr. Stewart promptly sent the papers back to Fr. Scheurmann, who performed the ceremony.

Around the mid nineties, I joined the Knights of St. Peter Claver Ladies Auxiliary, Presentation—Our Lady of Victory Court #189 and was treasurer for nearly eight years. I did not know of OLV's history with the Claver organization, because my parents were not involved in it during my childhood. My mother joined years later after the council reestablished itself in 1977. My research efforts and involvement as chairperson of the History Committee gave me the opportunity to learn about the council/court's rich history and humble beginnings at OLV.

I also had an opportunity to chaperone the Junior Daughters at their division conference in the spring of 2003 and was very impressed with the large turnout of black Catholic families. Mothers, fathers, and their children made the organization a family affair filling up a large block of the Birmingham, Alabama, hotel where we stayed. The southern hospitality was so refreshing. I had never seen so many black Catholics in one place in my life.

The Knights of St. Peter Claver has its roots in Alabama spreading to Louisiana, Texas, and many states throughout the country, and the organization is entrenched in the Catholic way of life. I was very impressed seeing fathers spending time with their sons as I took the girls in my charge swimming in the hotel pool.

Over the years, through people, and through this research project, I have learned of the black Catholic Church's strong presence in the southern states and the prominent role of the Knights of St. Peter Claver National in preserving that presence throughout the United States.

Both of my parents have passed on, and today, I am the only one left in my family who is a practicing Catholic. The next generation seems to have decided not to participate. Whose fault is it? One thing is certain, we cannot know where we are going if we don't know where we have been.

Growing up in Royal Oak Township. You can see the two-story
housing projects in background. Author is pictured with scarf around neck.

Connie's graduation, Mercy College, Detroit,
flanked by Mother, Joyce, and godmother, Martha.

Author's fourth grade class picture.

The shrill sound of the alarm clock as it calls them to serve an early Mass certainly has none of the glamour of bugle fanfare, but the altar boys of Our Lady of Victory are proud of the honor that is theirs. They are aware of the privilege it is to serve the Eucharistic King.

Do
It
For
God

Reprinted by permission from the Oblate Sisters of Providence Archives, Baltimore, Maryland. June—July 1959.

2002 All Schools Reunion sponsored by the Women's Club.
Vondie Curtis Hall is flanked by Mary and Wanda Robinson.

Author standing behind sisters Connie and Joyce.

Author with husband, Langston, at All Schools Reunion.

Clyde's high school graduation.

The Wall in Washington DC: A tribute to the soldiers killed in Viet Nam.

Lance Corporal Ronald L. Powell.

Renewal of wedding vows, April 2000.

II

The Pioneers

Introduction

Part II is a biographical compilation of the key pioneers who helped establish Our Lady of Victory. You will learn about Anna Bates, the founder of Our Lady of Victory, and Fr. Alvin Deem, first pastor and a missionary priest. You will learn about Fr. Hubert Roberge, who was the second pastor and first archdiocesan priest to serve in an all-black church. The Oblate Sisters of Providence were the black nuns out of Baltimore, Maryland, and they came to evangelize and start the new school. Msgr. Ferdinand DeCneudt was the next archdiocesan priest with a succession of priests to follow. The interviews with Almeta "Dolly" White and the Carter family will reveal priceless secrets.

You will learn the history of the early pioneers of the mission church. There were the board of directors of the Parish Credit Union; the appointed church committee men responsible for certifying all financial and annual reports and historical data. They include Thomas Lester, Riley Queen, Claude Carter, William Callis, Edward Wilson, Park R. Thornton, Conrad Gordon, Alvin R. Wrenn, John W. Luckett, Fred Carruth, Washington Leonard, and James Anderson.[1]

It is a fascinating account gathered from the archives, personal and telephone interviews, and photos. So enjoy!

Madre Anna Bates, Founder

Photo © Dwight Cendrowski

It is only fitting to talk about Anna Bates, since she is the reason that Our Lady of Victory ever came into existence. She was an unassuming person, certainly no one you would ever have expected to achieve greatness. Many of the members certainly did not realize her greatness until after she had passed, and a church wing was named after her. The church family called her Mother Bates or Madre Bates, whichever they preferred to use. She was small in stature, brown-skinned, and wore her hair pulled back in a bun and covered with a tam most of the time. She looked more like a Native-American. She had a high-pitched voice with a lyrical lilt.

She taught piano to the children in the church and in the surrounding community. When you entered her home, you always got a whiff of whatever had been cooking; the very strong, spicy smell permeated the entire house. It was a small, warm, cozy home. She taught piano lessons in her living room to all the children in the neighborhood, Catholic and other faiths. A daughter, Hazel Marie (called Marie by those who knew her), and a grandson, Clifford, lived with her, and they seemed to be a very tight-knit family. In the midsixties, Marie was in failing health and moved back home to be cared for by her mother. She died on March 9, 1967. Anna's son Keith passed away on August 1, 1978. Both of her children preceded her in death. It seemed so tragic at the time.

✝

Anna Bates was born in the West Indies in the early twentieth century. There is some conflicting information regarding the date and place of her birth. It has been recorded in various articles that she was born Anna Allen on December 26, 1904, in Bermuda. But research efforts of Philip Fortier, an Anna Bates fan, reveal that she was actually born on October 9, 1902, in Port of Spain, Trinidad, and it was believed that she grew up in Montserrat, another Caribbean island,[2] and arrived in Bermuda later on.

During Philip's many conversations with Anna Bates, he discovered that her maiden name, Allen, is an old family name from the island of Montserrat. Her family appears to have had a long legacy in that region.

In 1943, through her own tenacity, she founded a Catholic mission, Our Lady of Victory, in a little storefront on West Eight Mile Road and Cherrylawn Street in Detroit, Michigan. Even more impressive was that a mere three years later, this mission church moved into a facility built from the ground up for the West Eight Mile Community. A local merchant who had an interest in the development of the church and the area donated the land. The basement was dug and a donated structure trucked in and set on top of the foundation.

The usual migration patterns didn't fit what was happening in this little community. Normally, black folks took up residence in existing communities and took occupancy in existing Catholic churches that the white folks left behind when they moved out of the city. Building the church for black residents in the city of Detroit was a historic achievement and a tribute to the resourcefulness of this one little woman who persevered and made it happen. Madre Bates also founded the new church out of necessity since the nearest Catholic Church, Presentation on Meyers Road and Pembroke Street, did not welcome black folks.

Madre Bates immigrated to the United States, settling in Detroit when she was seventeen and living for over fifty years in Royal Oak Township. At some point in time, Madre Bates met and married Keith Smith and had two children, Hazel Marie and Keith Joseph. Her son and his wife, Daisy Smith, had seven children: Keith Joseph, Jacqueline, Ronald, Mark, Michael, Sonya, and Clifford. Mother Bates had nine great grandchildren. Daisy resides in the vicinity of the Madonna parish in Detroit.

There is no information about her marriage to Keith, only that the marriage broke down and they parted ways. She met and married a minister, the Rev. Cassius Clay Bates, who was living in Royal Oak Township. Then she started going to St. James Catholic Church on Nine Mile and Woodward in Ferndale. According to Daisy, her mother-in-law walked until it got to be too much to cover the approximate five-mile distance going and coming every week.

Those familiar with the area can tell you that walking from Royal Oak Township to St. James was a tremendous undertaking. To do it each Sunday was surely a test of one's faith. Daisy said that was about the time that her mother-in-law started conducting religious instruction in a storefront on her own before Father Alvin Deem was assigned. Mother Bates contacted Sr. Ann Molony at Marygrove to help her get started and kept calling the diocese for a priest. Daisy had no memory of Sr. Ann's last name but research efforts of Richard Smith turned up Molony as the probable name.

Madre Anna Bates saw the large number of children in the neighborhood and envisioned a parish with a school to educate them. That explains her contacts with Marygrove College, where the nuns of the Immaculate Heart of Mary (IHM) were living. However, because she was the only Catholic in the area, their response was not too encouraging. Instead, the sisters referred her to Msgr. John Ryan, director of the Confraternity of Christian Doctrine of the Archdiocese of Detroit. Again, because there were so few Catholics in the area, Msgr. Ryan could give no assurances that a church would ever be built.

Madre Bates was not ready to give up on her vision. She saw a need for the church's presence in a protestant community in order to win new souls. That was in direct opposition to Msgr. Ryan's position that there had to be Catholics to justify a church in that West Eight Mile Community. Just imagine this little woman calling the diocese on a regular basis. It took guts and courage to do it in that time of racial discrimination. The diocese could not continue to ignore her. She wouldn't let them.

With Madre Bates's encouragement, Sr. Mary from Marygrove College convinced Shelton Johnson, director of Birdhurst Recreation Center, to allow the sisters to use the center for a summer school program. In the beginning, there were seventy to eighty children. As word spread, the numbers grew.

On June 25, 1945, summer school opened, and four IHM sisters and the administrator found 350 children waiting for them. As Madre Bates had predicted, many children came for the classes, which included religious instruction. Some of them had to be sent back home with notes stating that there were not enough teachers to handle the large number of children that day. Mother Teresa sent two more sisters from the motherhouse in Monroe to help out immediately. When the summer ended, the parents' enthusiasm did not. They wanted the sisters to continue a program of instruction and to hold classes for adults, as well. Edward Dickens of the Wyman School Board made a building available to teach the classes. Events moved quickly as attendance continued to grow.

In the second year of the program, again living at Marygrove, the sisters were joined by Sr. Ann Maloney, and another nun, Sr. Juletta. Later, they would be joined by other sisters as well as students from Marygrove and, together with the dedicated laity, would lay the strong foundation for the close-knit community of Our Lady of Victory.

✝

In the fall of 1943, Archbishop Edward Mooney asked the Franciscans of the Cincinnati Province to open a mission for the community at Eight Mile Road. Fr. Alvin Deem, who arrived at Duns Scotus College in Southfield earlier that summer, quickly volunteered for the project. Msgr. Ryan obtained the store at West Eight Mile and Cherrylawn, which a group of seminarians and brothers from Duns Scotus painted and repaired. When completed, the new mission was christened Our Lady of Victory. Through the determination and vision of one formidable woman, Fr. Alvin Deem celebrated the first Mass in the mission on the Feast of St. Francis of Assisi in 1943.[3]

Mother Anna Bates helped Fr. Alvin recruit the McKenzie family. They were one of the first pioneer families who were baptized and received their first Holy Communion on May 28, 1944.

Fr. Alvin was moving very quickly to get a new church and school, because it was becoming very crowded trying to keep Mass down to one service on Sundays. If the archdiocese had acted in a timely manner, perhaps the land that had increased in value from $800 to $7,500 could be purchased, anyway. Indeed, Fr. Alvin wrote to Msgr. Ryan that the money was there. He indicated in his letter, dated March 12, 1945, that the people in the area had money and jobs. He made it clear that the money was there to start the process of building the church and school. He had his pulse on the community and tried to convey that to the archdiocese. This is part of a letter in which he discussed the cost fluctuation of the land:

> I wish you would please tell His Grace before the final decision is made, that I think it will be possible for the Mission to pay the $5,000—no, make it $4,000—by June 1 instead of the $2,000.00 I mentioned in the last letter and the December date. It is possible that by December we could pay the whole balance between the $800 price once promised and the actual cost of $7,500.[4]

Of course, the archdiocese did not act on Fr. Alvin's recommendation, so an opportunity was missed to acquire land for the church and school in that year of 1945.

As it turned out, the new church building was erected in 1946. The school was built eight years later, and Anna Bates became known as the founder of Our Lady of Victory Mission. Her interest in evangelizing Catholicism and her concern for the education of children never ceased. Wherever there was a religious, educational, musical, or cultural gathering, she was there.

The residents of the West Eight Mile Community became familiar with the sight of Fr. Alvin and Mother Bates walking, visiting, and enlisting converts for the Catholic Church. Mother Bates remained a source of inspiration and strength in the community until the day of her death on May 23, 1983. OLV Mission named its social hall Madre Bates Hall, in a tribute to her memory, and the name carried over to Presentation's west wing after the merger in 1975. She was a woman of great faith and a role model to her community.

According to Philip, there had been, among people who were familiar with her work, some talk of elevating Madre Anna Bates to the status of sainthood after she was laid to rest. Certainly, she figured prominently in the history of black Catholic affairs in the city, and many people recognized her holiness.

Father Alvin Deem

Assigned 1943–1946

Franciscan archives, Cincinnati,
Province of St. John Baptist

With the celebration of Father Alvin Deem's Golden Jubilee on Sunday, October 21, 1990, we will explore the beginnings of Our Lady of Victory Mission Church and his key contributions to its history. Here is an article prepared by Fr. Joseph Gagnon, who was the presiding priest of the merged Presentation—Our Lady of Victory Church:

This month the Nobel Peace Prize was given to Mikhail Gorbachev, president of the Soviet Union, for opening the door to political freedoms in Eastern Europe. Some have minimized his effort, contending that he only did the obvious before it was too late. Such minimizing would be credible, except that nobody else had the courage to do what was obvious.

Similarly, Fr. Alvin Deem, a Franciscan priest, did no big thing by ministering among African Americans living in the vicinity of Eight Mile Road and Wyoming from 1943 to 1946. He visited a lot of people in their homes, evangelized and taught the Christian Catholic faith to new converts, taught a lot of children, arranged for religious sisters (Oblate Sisters of Providence) to teach in a Catholic school, formed a strong evangelization team to extend and to continue the ministry of Christ, and celebrated life in the sacraments with all who came. His method was not particularly novel. Other priests could have done as much.

The point is, of course, that nobody else did. Even worse, people seeking instruction and membership in the Catholic Church were turned away by local priests. Few in the church seemed to understand the situation. So when one priest understood, and then acted to evangelize and establish a Christian Catholic community among a people rejected by established parishes, it took real guts. He deserves a prize.

We do not give Father Alvin Deem the Nobel Peace Prize. We do give him our love, appreciation, and heartfelt thanks. His name will be bold in the Book of Life written by the Eternal Prince of Peace.

Curiously, the name chosen for the mission was Our Lady of Victory. To put the new mission under the same patronage as Presentation of Our Lady Parish brought Mary, the Mother of the Lord, prominently into the picture. I am sure she helped bring the two together.

Peace,

Fr. Joseph Gagnon, Pastor[5]

On October 21, 1990, Father Alvin returned to the merged Presentation—Our Lady of Victory Church to celebrate his Golden Jubilee (fifty years in the priesthood). Many of the original members of Our Lady of Victory were there to greet him. At the time of this jubilee celebration, Presentation—Our Lady of Victory had around 400 families and an elementary school.

The jubilee included a celebration Mass, a procession to the statue of Our Lady of Victory, the releasing of balloons, and a reception. Various committees of Presentation—Our Lady of Victory coordinated the Golden Jubilee to honor Fr. Alvin Deem who came back for the celebration and to reminisce with old friends. Another well-loved priest in attendance was Msgr. Ferdinand DeCneudt the third pastor to lead Our Lady of Victory.

✝

Fr. Alvin Deem was born in New Albany, Indiana, on April 17, 1913. He was ordained as a Franciscan in 1940. Aside from one year as a chaplain in Peoria, Illinois, and one year teaching at Roger Bacon High School in Cincinnati, the whole of his fifty-two years of active ministry was in parishes. He spent forty-eight years in "pioneer ministry" to African Americans, beginning with the founding of the storefront church of Our Lady of Victory in 1943. Though he served only three years as founding pastor, his contribution to the archdiocese had such impact that in 1988, Edmund Cardinal Szoka named him recipient of the Archdiocese of Detroit's Crusader Award. From Detroit, he moved to St. Joseph Parish on the Paseo in Kansas City, Missouri, where he served for sixteen years. In 1963, he moved to the Mississippi Delta where he spent twenty-nine years as pastor at St. Jude Church in Diamond, Louisiana. Fr. Alvin was strong and vocal in his opinions but always gracious in expressing them.[6]

Being vocal but gracious may have put Fr. Alvin at odds with his superiors in the fight to help blacks achieve the American dream, and he had simply found a way to voice his opinions without offending. Getting along with the archdiocese is everything when you are on a mission as formidable as the one he had undertaken.

Fr. Alvin came to Detroit and took up residence at Duns Scotus College. Detroit was a city troubled by racial unrest. Although the Diocese of Detroit was responsible for ministering to the entire community, it neglected the enclave of African Americans living in Royal Oak Township and Detroit bordered by West Eight Mile Road. Moreover, African Americans were not welcome at the surrounding Catholic parishes.

Late in 1943, and shortly after the race riots, Fr. Alvin began his ministry in the abandoned storefront on the corner of Cherrylawn and West Eight Mile Road. He commuted from Duns Scotus College, three miles distant, while organizing the mission. He rented a small store, and, with help and donations from neighbors and potential parishioners, the mission was cleaned and renovated. Our Lady of Victory Mission formally opened with the offering of the first Mass on October 3, 1943. Two babies were baptized that day. Although the neighborhood was practically 100 percent non-Catholic at the time of his arrival, Fr. Alvin baptized seventy-eight people during the three years of his administration.

Fr. Alvin's deep commitment to the community, especially to the children, was evident. He evangelized from door-to-door in his brown, heavy robe, white cord, bare feet, and sandals. He taught the Catholic faith and offered Mass. He encouraged the youth to get a good education and helped many of them attend Catholic schools. He secured jobs and college scholarships for many of the young adults.

Respect for Fr. Alvin and his work was so great that he was able to convince "Doc" Washington, a local tavern owner, to donate land on the corner of Washburn and Eight Mile Road for a new church. Fr. Alvin invited some sisters from Baltimore, and the church began to take shape as the venerable institution it would eventually become. During his brief stay at Our Lady of Victory, he laid a strong foundation and had a deep impact on the neighboring community. New homes were built around the parish. This was the beginning of an African American Catholic Community. His contributions helped to strengthen the foundation of an entire black community.

In 1944, OLV was consecrated, built primarily with the labor of members of the mission church. Fr. Alvin, with the Oblate Sisters of Providence, continued his ministry of home visits and evangelization to make plans for establishing a school.

✝

During most of 1945, Fr. Alvin spent his time imploring the diocese to give him more space, as he was bulging at the seams in the storefront church. The parishioners had painted and repaired the storefront. Their numbers soon outgrew the limited space that was cramped with a makeshift altar and seats that were provided for the members.

There were 300 children receiving religious education at that time. This was more than enough to justify building a school. He wrote to Msgr. John C. Ryan on March 12, March 16, and June 25, 1945—three separate occasions—trying to get church and school. The tone of those letters may have been a source of irritation for the archdiocese. They started taking a closer look at who had authority over Our Lady of Victory Mission. Was it the Franciscans or the archdiocese? The Rev. Ryan wrote to His Eminence Edward Cardinal Mooney addressing his concerns over the fact that nowhere was it mentioned that the Franciscan Order acknowledges the diocese's authority over the mission church and that the matter had to be corrected.[7]

In the meantime, Fr. Alvin, unaware of what was coming, was happily corresponding with the Rev. Ryan regarding his preparations and his anticipation of moving to the newly built church. He describes the items he had obtained such as candlesticks, altar, tabernacle, vases, founts, statues, drapes, and a donated Kilgen organ—all the items needed to furnish a new church. The letter clearly shows Fr. Alvin's excitement and anticipation of the big move to the new church and the extent to which he was preparing to make it happen. After all, he had worked hard to make this day possible. This was his project. He had no idea what was about to happen.[8]

Msgr. Ryan wrote to the Very Rev. Romauld Mollaun, OFM, at the direction of His Eminence Cardinal Mooney, stating that the archdiocese now had a priest to take over OLV Mission.[9] This act was certainly unprecedented given the history of the archdiocese in not assigning its personnel to black churches. The fact that it happened this time was not to bode well for Our Lady of Victory.

Rev. Herbert Klosterkemper, OFM, wrote to the Rev. Edward Hickey that effective October 22, 1946, Fr. Alvin had been instructed to leave his assignment at OLV Mission.[10] The chancellor's office seemed very concerned about Fr. Alvin's feelings in this turn of events and expressed it to Rev. Klosterkemper, O.F.M:

> I am grateful for the very courteous and prompt action you have taken in recalling Father Alvin Deem from Our Lady of Victory Mission, Detroit. I sincerely hope that this action does not have the effect of seriously discouraging Father Alvin, because I believe he was deeply interested, enthusiastic, and zealous in his devotion to the work among the colored.[11]

However, what the chancellor failed to realize was that the parishioners were deeply affected by this move, so much so that a number of them left the mission.

Fr. Alvin had a strong impact on the neighboring community. He ran the mission on the premise that all people were entitled to respect and dignity. It must have hurt him terribly to have to leave before his work was done.

Perhaps if he had been allowed to stay for a little while, he would have left a much larger church and would have been able to encourage more young black men to pursue the priesthood or other religious affiliations. Certainly, all the signs were there.

Fr. Alvin also had lofty dreams of building a hospital to serve the area, because it was desperately needed. He wanted to do so many wonderful things for the black community. However, he was not able to see his dream become a reality because of his sudden departure.

He grew up seeing the effects of racism. There was a history of slave ownership within his family. Sharecropping was not that much different from slavery; blacks were not able to amass their fortune during the mid-twentieth century even though slavery had been abolished with the signing of the Emancipation Proclamation over a century earlier. Having lived around blacks on his family's plantation and having gained a deeper understanding of their plight, it's easy to see why Fr. Alvin could work so well within the black community and why he had so little patience with the establishment.

On October 26, 1946, a new chapel was erected on a permanent site at 10113 West Eight Mile Road with a dedication by Edward Cardinal Mooney. On that day, Fr. Hubert Roberge replaced Fr. Alvin.

The Reverend Alvin Deem, longtime pastor in African American Catholic communities passed away at the age of eighty-five on Saturday, August 15, 1998, on the sixty-eighth anniversary of his investiture as a friar at the Franciscan at St. Clare Retirement Community. Father Deem left behind several nieces and nephews and was buried at St. Mary Cemetery in St. Bernard, Ohio.[6] And he also left behind to mourn him a parish family in Detroit.

Father Hubert Roberge

Assigned 1946–1953

Fr. Hubert Roberge was the first archdiocesan priest to head an all-black parish, and he was the second priest to be assigned to Our Lady of Victory. Because of the historical significance, Fr. Roberge recorded and emphasized this fact in the Historical Data section of the financial records on Oct. 26, 1946.

His niece, Anne Purvis, submitted this family history on her "Uncle Bert" as the family affectionately called him:

> He was born in Michigan after his parents migrated here from Quebec. Their names were Louis Alfred Roberge and Anastasia Mercure. I have the

51

paperwork that states that the Roberge's lived in Flanders, France in the 1300s. Father Roberge had five siblings, including Father Leo Roberge, who also was a priest in the Archdiocese of Detroit.

Father Bert was buried at Mt. Olivet Cemetery. After my own father passed away in 1958, he (Father Roberge) became the "official" head of our family, and we always were together on special occasions.

His final assignment was chaplain at Lourdes Nursing Home (near Clarkston) when he had a stroke and became totally dependent. That didn't stop him. He would show up at our door for special occasions in an ambulance with an attendant who would take care of his personal needs during his visit. My fondest memory was when he was at our family home for Christmas dinner and he said, "I hear Paul!" Paul was my older brother, now deceased. We said, "No, Uncle Bert, Paul is on his way home from Vietnam and not expected for another two weeks." He firmly told me to go out and look out front. Paul was dropped off at the nearest exit of Interstate 94 and was walking up to the house.

Uncle Bert was very strict but loving. He often said his favorite assignment was at Our Lady of Victory. He said the parishioners were good, hardworking individuals who believed in Our Lord and worked together to achieve their goals.[12]

The priests of those days were sometimes drawn to a life of spirituality and more visible roles, modeling their lives on those of missionary priests who were so popular in the minds of clergy. Fr. Hubert Roberge captured this spirituality as a kind of missionary archdiocesan priest. He left Detroit in the early years of his career to serve for a time in the Diocese of Mobile, Alabama, at a small and poor mission for the city's blacks. He returned to the archdiocese in 1943, and was one of the first diocesan priests to work in Detroit's black community. It took a great deal of courage to alert his fellow clergy to the festering problem of racial discrimination in the city, but by doing so, he helped them toward a more spiritual fulfillment of the priesthood.[13]

While assigned to Our Lady of Victory, he became the chaplain for the newly organized Knights of St. Peter Claver, Santa Maria Council #105 and worked extensively with Luther Keith. He also gave Keith assignments to find property for the Archdiocese of Detroit, which was always looking for land for new expansions.

He added the rectory and convent and was working on the school building when he left, paving the way for the next priest. Fr. Roberge was photographed with approximately seventy-six first communicants before a school was built, which was a phenomenal achievement in itself. He came back to support the first graduating class of 1960.

He was known for his tasteful and exquisite decorating and designing talents, which were evident in the beauty of the church interior. Pictures could not capture the true beauty and simplicity of OLV.

A statue of the Blessed Mother Mary was placed on the left side of the altar facing the congregation, and a statue of St. Martin DePorres was placed on the right side. He was a black saint, and it seemed only fitting for the statue to be in an all-black church. The parishioners must have derived some sort of comfort gazing at the statue of St. Martin DePorres since there was little exposure to black saints.

There was a large crucifix hanging above the center of the altar. There was an altar rail where parishioners knelt to receive communion. Simple stained-glass windows lined the right and left sides of the church. Parishioners sat on wooden pews with kneelers. The shiny, tiled floor always smelled of wax. Lighted candles and the smell of incense made the atmosphere welcoming. You felt peace and warmth just being there.

✝

It was a fact that the Catholic Church in the early days of Detroit was administered along racial lines. This age-old problem had surfaced during the apostolic times when St. Paul confronted Peter and the college of apostles on their treatment of the gentile converts.[14]

Tentler states that by the late 1940s, Cardinal Mooney had begun to think in terms of an integrated church. He never condemned segregation, and he tolerated it from some of his parish schools. Chancery sympathies in the post-war years were leaning towards those priests who were interested in the "Negro Apostolate" and who were prepared to integrate their parishes and schools. Fr. Hubert Roberge, who came to St. Leo after leaving OLV, assumed correctly that he had Mooney's full support in his efforts to make St. Leo a model of racial cooperation.

Blacks had been attending the church for a number of years when Roberge became pastor. St. Leo High School had been the first in Detroit to integrate, as far back as the late 1930s. They were using "quotas" back in those days. But in the 1950s, there were still no black members in the various parish organizations. Fr. Roberge set out to correct this imbalance. He integrated the ushers and the Altar Society. He appointed a black parishioner to the church committee, and lectured his congregation on the virtues of treating one another as spiritual brothers and sisters in Christ's mystical body.

Cardinal Mooney, while pleased by the progress at St. Leo, was alarmed when he learned that Fr. Roberge made a public appeal in a 1954 article for an official statement from the American bishops against racism and continued segregation in the church. The work at St. Leo was supposed to have proceeded quietly and with an understanding that there would be no publicity.[15]

Luckily, for OLV, Fr. Roberge was the right priest at the time, since his appointment had come so quickly. However, after seven years, he, too, was gone.

When Fr. Roberge took up his assignment at St. Leo, the parents of Our Lady of Victory enrolled their teens in the high school there knowing they would be in good care. That was his legacy.

The Oblate Sisters of Providence

July 2, 2004, marked the 175th Anniversary of the founding of the Oblate Sisters of Providence. A Mass and reception/dinner took place in downtown Baltimore. The motherhouse is at 701 Gun Road in Baltimore, Maryland. This historic black religious teaching order of nuns staffed Our Lady of Victory School, and this is their story.

Fr. James Joubert was a Sulpician teaching at St. Mary's Seminary. He established St. Frances School for Colored Girls (later called St. Frances Academy) in Baltimore with the aid of several young black women—all with ties to the San Domingue (present day Haiti) refugee community. The four women eventually founded the Oblate Sisters of Providence through the support of Fr. Joubert. Elizabeth Lange, Marie Magdalene Bales, Rosine Boegue, and Theresa Duchemin Maxis formed the first religious community of black sisters in the United States, and probably in the world, on July 2, 1829. By 1962, the sisters staffed thirty schools in fifteen states. Their more than 300 members came from most of the fifty states and from seven Latin American countries. Their principal work was teaching, but the sisters also engaged in sewing, catechetical work, lay retreats, and homes for the dependent children.[16]

Sr. Theresa Maxis was born of refugee parents from Santo Domingo. Many families fled Santo Domingo, Haiti, and other colonies of France and Spain in the nineteenth century. On their arrival here, they discovered a situation not all that much better than what they had left. Sr. Theresa was elected superior for what was to be the most difficult years of the order. It was not easy for a group of black Catholic women to move and live in a border state two decades before the Emancipation Proclamation was signed.

According to Sr. M. Rosalita in *No Greater Service*, a chronicle of the IHM Sisters, Sr. Theresa Maxis left the Oblates in 1845, seeking to join a more established community. Instead, a Redemptorist priest from Michigan, Fr. Louis Gillet, convinced her to come with him to Monroe to work in a school at St. Mary's Parish with another group of women. She was having some reservations about the fate of the Oblate Sisters, who were receiving so little support and welcomed the opportunity to move somewhere else where she found support.

Detroit Free Press columnist Desiree Cooper wrote that when Mother Theresa came to Monroe, Michigan, she left behind her black identity, as she was biracial and could very easily pass for white. She became the first superior of the Sisters Servants of the Immaculate Heart of Mary (IHM).

There was some controversy in her life after a move to establish the IHMs in Scranton, Pennsylvania, and she was banned from the order in later years, because she was considered a troublemaker by her Superiors. She lived sixteen years of her life in exile with the Grey Nuns in Ottawa, Canada. She had no contact with the IHMs during this time, as she was completely severed from them. When she did return, she went to Pennsylvania and was never allowed to return to the motherhouse in Monroe, Michigan again. Marygrove College in Detroit evolved from St. Mary Academy, which Mother Theresa established with forty students in 1846.[17]

Today, Marygrove has a Senior Citizen's Complex that bears Mother Theresa Maxis's name.[18] Because of an attempt by the church to hide her racial identity and her membership in the all-black Oblates, there was not much information readily available on Mother Theresa Maxis. Thanks to the tenacity of Desiree Cooper for uncovering the mystery of Mother Theresa's life. Mother Theresa may finally get the recognition she surely deserves. Her place in history with her role in the establishment of the Oblate Sisters of Providence and the IHMs will finally be recognized.

The Oblates, founded in 1829, and the IHMs, founded in 1845, and later Immaculata and Scranton, founded in Pennsylvania, share a common interest and have taken steps to remember their common roots. As noted on their Web site, they came together in July 2005 to celebrate and remember. The Oblate/IHM Logo *Many Stories, One Heart 2005*, sums up who they are.

Shortly after the Reverend James Joubert assumed the position of catechist in the Chapelle Basse, Elizabeth Lange learned with joy that her ten-year longing to be a religious sister could be fulfilled. Becoming Sister Mary, she made her first promises along with three companions, on July 2, 1829, and at that time was already in her early forties. She lived with her religious sisters for a total of fifty-four years, serving as superior general from 1829 to 1832 and from 1835 to 1841. She died on Friday, February 3, 1882.[19]

Father Joubert was a practical, determined, eminently spiritual man, who had both feet on the ground at all times. He stood boldly against his many contemporaries who were holding that blacks had neither souls to be saved or minds to be instructed.

Father Joubert constantly had to get around the slavery system by acting as both slave owner and slave seller. An example of this was explained by George Anderson. One document written in Fr. Joubert's own hand, certifies that he "sets free from bondage my negro girl Angelica Gideon, who is about fourteen years of age." But his action was, in fact, a maneuver to circumvent the slavery system. He had purchased Angelica and then freed her in order to ensure that she could attend the St. Frances Academy as a free African-American child. His act thus forestalled any possible questions as to her status as free or slave. Angelica later entered the congregation as Sister Mary Angelica. The order was in danger of shutting down upon Fr. Joubert's death in 1843, because the archbishop saw little point in continuing the education of black children. But St. Frances Academy did survive and thrive. A coed student body of 300 currently occupies the Academy, and it is still in its nineteenth-century location on East Chase Street in Baltimore. Mother Lange's simplistic bedroom is preserved there.

The Oblate Sisters have a foreign mission in Costa Rica, and some of the Costa Rican nuns are working in Florida; other Oblates are in Buffalo, New

York, with the rest in Baltimore, working at the Academy, teaching in local parochial schools and ministering in three local parishes.[20]

At the time of their 150th Anniversary Celebration, the Oblates were in various parts of the United States including Our Lady of Victory in Detroit. In later years, a few nuns were sent to some Detroit area suburban parishes—Livonia and Three Rivers, Michigan.

✝

Soon after Archbishop Mooney had asked the Franciscans to serve the parish at OLV, one of Fr. Alvin's first decisions was to travel to Baltimore and request that the mother superior of the Oblate Sisters send sisters to Our Lady of Victory. It was only after Fr. Roberge continued the case for bringing the sisters to Detroit that it finally happened. Although the mother superior protested that she had no one available, and all the glitches had to be worked out, by the fall of 1948, the sisters appeared. The only impediment was a statement in the contract that said the sisters would have to visit homes and take up census. However, these nuns were not allowed to visit homes and would have to get permission from the ecclesiastical superior, Msgr. Harry A. Quinn of Baltimore, to relax the rules. Fr. Roberge was determined that this impediment would not stand in the way of the Oblates coming to Detroit. He hoped that they would use this opportunity to spread the word of Christ, which he felt was what the order ought to be about anyway.

In 1948, Sr. Mary Augustine Green arrived as the youngest member of a convent of four sisters. The others were Sr. Mary Patricia Ford, Sr. Mary of Nazareth Johnson, and Mother Providencia Pollard. Sisters M. Trinita and M. Concetta replaced Sisters Patricia and Mary of Nazareth later on. Sr. Augustine recalls that they were well received at most of the homes they visited during the census, which they took in that first year. Through this work, the nuns became very familiar with the community in which they were to live.

They stayed with the IHM sisters at Most Holy Trinity Convent until work on their convent was completed. Two lots had been purchased earlier that same year to build their convent.

While awaiting the day the school would open, the nuns did home visits. They also engaged in catechetical instruction of children and women. Children were coming two afternoons per week for classes in the basement of

OLV Church. Sr. Augustine recalled an active parish with numerous activities and events.

Rev. John C. Ryan noted in a letter to the Rev. John A. Donovan that the nuns had to get special dispensation of the ecclesiastical superior before he could allow them to do parish visiting on a temporary basis until the school was established, since this community was strictly a community of trained teachers. Rev. Ryan also had recommended that the nuns be engaged to open St. George's School in the fall of 1948 if that parish was to become a colored mission.[21] Of course, this recommendation never materialized.

The pastor, Fr. Hubert Roberge, had recently returned from two years of work in Birmingham, Alabama, and Marygrove students continued to assist with music for the Masses and other religious services. The sisters were completely involved in the parish community. Often they would accompany a young woman about to be married on a shopping trip to buy material for her wedding dress and would direct the practice for the wedding itself.[22] By the year 1950, a record number of 106 baptisms and 63 converts were the fruit of bringing the Oblates into the apostolate. This evangelization laid the groundwork for the mission church.

The habit that the Oblate Sisters of Providence wore changed from the cap to a black veil in 1906. Mother Mary Patrick Ward of the Sisters of the Humility of Mary assisted the Oblates in the new headgear. She designed a veil similar to the one worn by her order. The veil was a starched, rectangular, muslin piece-called a domino-sewn under the head section of the veil, which was folded back five inches. This part was in turn pinned to a band or crown with three straight black pins, one at each side and the third in the middle forming a dip or bend in the front. Under the veil the sisters donned a face piece which hid their hair and ears entirely. In 1906, four Oblate Sisters modeled the new veil for Cardinal Gibbons, the archbishop of Baltimore. He quickly gave his approval for the new veil. This headdress was worn for a full fifty years after its adoption, with no alteration except the ironing in of extra starched pieces to keep the domino stiff. A rounded starched white linen guimpe and collar was now worn over the top front of the long dresses.

The habit proper was all one piece until in 1956 the one piece dress changed to a skirt and blouse. The black apron was eliminated at this time also. Excessive hand sewing was forbidden and as much of the stitching as possible was now done by machine. Sleeves were shaped and much tighter. The veil was changed once again in August 1962. At the time the sisters discarded the starched linen domino with the pinned "dip" for an inch and a half in width strip of plastic veilboard, that was inserted into the front hem of the black veil. The pliable veilboard gave the veil its frontal shape. Now there would be no more pinning of the veil to the crown, instead the veil would be snapped with snap fasteners to the crown which was also plastic. The sisters experimented with the use of plastic guimpes and band for several years prior. The object was to lighten the load of the laundress as well as to improve uniformity in dress of the Oblates.[16]

✝

Dolly said that in the old days the nuns went door-to-door to recruit children for the school. That school never could have been completed without those nuns who arrived before the ground was broken. She recalls a group called Friends of the Oblates. They used to give teas and bake sales to raise money for the mother house.

Gloria Cook, another pioneer recalled the group name as the Oblate Sisters of Providence Guild. She remembers the guild going to Washington DC; touring Baltimore, Maryland; and having teas on Woodward Avenue to raise money. The teas were held at the Great Lakes Building, which was a popular place to hold functions at the time. Although memories differ, the goal was the same, to raise money to support the Oblates.

According to Dolly, the Friends of the Oblates kept the church basement clean because the janitor couldn't do it all. Her mother, Almeta Carruth, was in charge of doing the laundry for the nuns. Dolly describes a gadget called a mangle. It is about table-length with a big, padded roller on it. The same devices were used in the cleaning and pressing shops.

She said, "You put your garment on one of those, and it would roll over the big roller and iron itself out, and that was progress rather than standing there doing it by hand. My job was to press those collars the nuns wore around their necks. You got your iron and put the garment on the dry part. That part got wet, so you'd pick it up and turn and move it over to a dry side. Many hands kept those garments clean, and it was done once a week. You could go in the basement of the convent, but they wouldn't let you through the front door."

Almeta was the president of the Oblate Sisters of Providence Guild in the late fifties and was featured in the *Oblate News and Views* Jun-Jul 1959 issue. The Oblate Sisters published the magazine bimonthly at their Baltimore,

Maryland, location to fund the motherhouse. Here is a heartwarming reprint from the April–May 1961 issue:

"Oblates a Refuge in Adversity"
By Margaret Murphy

Condensed from The Michigan Catholic

The knock came hesitantly on the back door of the convent. "Mrs. Jones" had gotten a call for day work and, unable to turn down the needed income, left her three youngsters in bed with the sniffles, with the stern admonition to "go right to the sisters" if anything went wrong.

Now the three of them—in pajamas, robes, and slippers—accompanied by their pet dog and cat, stood at the door and solemnly explained mother's orders and their problem.

Their house was on fire and what should they do? Sister, of course, herded them into the warm kitchen and called the fire department. Sister Patricia, OSP chuckled as she recalled the amusing but significant incident.

In 1943, when Our Lady of Victory parish started at Eight Mile and Wyoming to serve an all-Negro area, there were less than ten Catholic families. There are now almost two hundred. First masses were offered in a neighborhood social hall, and later in a store building on Eight Mile Road, with the Reverend Alvin T. Deem, OFM, pastor.

By the time of the second pastor, the Reverend Hubert Roberge, the old church of another Detroit parish had been purchased and moved to its new site on Eight Mile Road. Steady progress since has increased the parishioners to 185 families. Following Father Roberge came the Reverend Ferdinand DeCneudt and the present pastor, the Reverend Raymond Maiberger.

Our Lady of Victory School was the latest addition to the parish plant, conducted by the Oblate Sisters who came to the parish in 1948. The original five-room school opened in 1954, and has increased to nine classrooms plus offices. There are now 224 students from kindergarten to eighth grade.

What has the coming of the church meant to the neighborhood? Father Maiberger can answer that. He points to the homes—neat, well tended, most of them new. Fifteen years ago the homes were dilapidated, jerry-built. The new homes in most cases are being paid for by the hard work of both mother and father, but they are helped along a unified family life among parishioners.

Change in the crime rate, says Fr. Maiberger, has been miraculous. He credits the radical change to the influence of the school, particularly on family life, the impact of the faith, and a growing community of self-respect and pride.

On September 6, 1948, Fr. Hubert Roberge noted the arrival of the Oblate Sisters of Providence as the first order of black nuns to work in the archdiocese. The nuns were role models for black girls in the neighborhood as they represented an alternative occupation.

Sr. Sharon Young, OSP expressed a desire to become a religious sister at a very early age. She came from a big family and she learned to love and respect the church in early childhood. She left Our Lady of Victory in 1954 and attended St. Leo High School, which was run by the Sisters of Charity. In 1956, she entered the order of the Oblate Sisters of Providence.[23]

Dolly's mother was instrumental in getting Sr. Sharon's dowry together for her trip to Baltimore. She had a couple of showers for her as well. A nun is considered a bride of Christ, and so having a dowry was similar to the gifts that a bride brings to her husband to be.

Mother Stella Marie, OSP, the beautiful mother superior, arrived and taught third and fourth grades at Our Lady of Victory in the fall of 1955. She taught the pupils how to sing in Latin for the High Mass on Sunday, and she organized the Junior Sodality Girls. Mother Stella Marie and the other nuns on staff at the school prepared the children for baptism and their first Holy Communion. They also helped the children learn their catechism lessons well. She died of a brain tumor at the motherhouse in Baltimore many years ago. She will always be remembered by those who were privileged to know her.

Mother Mary Patricia Ford, OSP, was one of the original Oblates—the Fabulous Four—coming back home. Her story appeared in Our Lady of Victory Church Bulletin on June 16, 1963:

> Mother Patricia first came to Our Lady of Victory as Sister Patricia in 1948. She gave private adult instructions, catechized groups of children, and conducted choir practice, which formed the foundation of the parish's strength. After five years, she left Our Lady of Victory to serve in Chicago, where she celebrated her silver jubilee as an Oblate Sister. From Chicago, she was transferred to Baltimore, Maryland.
>
> In 1957, Detroit reclaimed Mother Mary Patricia as superior and principal of Our Lady of Victory School. She taught sixth through eighth grades. Mother updated and modernized the school. She prepared the first graduating class of 1960 for the commencement ceremony.

In 1962, Mother Patricia began learning how to drive so that she could take over the new station wagon, donated by a generous benefactor, Fr. Eppenbrock, at St. Timothy's Parish in Trenton.

The original nuns who staffed Our Lady of Victory after construction was completed included Mother Providencia replacing Mother Patricia; Sr. DePaul, Sr. Virgine, Sr. Teresita, and Sr. Stephana. Then the next year, Mother Stella Marie arrived and stayed two years. Mother Patricia returned and was the longest serving Mother Superior at the school.

In the Appendix is a list of all the Oblates who served at Our Lady of Victory and Presentation. Those who served after the merger have an asterisk behind their name. Some are deceased now, and those who are no longer Oblates have a double asterisk. A sincere effort was made to try to be as accurate as possible.

Reverend Ferdinand DeCneudt

Assigned 1953–1959

Msgr. Ferdinand DeCneudt wrote his autobiography from memory for a couple of religious publications. Now Our Lady of Victory's members will learn a little bit more about this priest who left his mark on the mission church.

Msgr. DeCneudt was born on September 23, 1912, in the town of Ghent, Belgium. He was the youngest and only son of four siblings. On July 4, 1920, when he was eight years old, his family arrived in the United States. After spending hours on Ellis Island, they boarded a train headed for Detroit,

Michigan. He attended St. Margaret Mary School on the east side of Detroit and graduated in June 1927. He went to Cass Technical High School his freshman year and transferred to the newly opened Catholic Central High School the next year. Some time along the way, he made a conscious decision to become a priest, and after graduation, he was driven to Sacred Heart Seminary on Thanksgiving Day 1931.

His first assignment in 1939 was as assistant pastor at St. Elizabeth in Wyandotte, Michigan. In September 1942, he received his next assignment at the Church of Our Lady of Sorrows on Meldrum and Benson Streets in Detroit. This parish had a mixed congregation that included Italians, Lebanese, and blacks. The area looked too commercial for his tastes, and initially he was not happy being there, but soon he settled in and had a great relationship with the pastor, Fr. Frank Van Hout.

The sudden death of his father changed everything in an instant. His father died of a heart attack while at work in the paint shop of Borden's Creamery. He was sixty-four years old and planning his retirement. Fr. DeCneudt was unable to get to him in time even though he was only five minutes away. That had to be a devastating time for him. His mother was left a widow and lived twenty-seven more years before she died at the age of ninety-two.

DeCneudt received an invitation to teach at the University of Detroit. He handled large numbers of students and returning GIs, teaching two classes, twice a week, back to back, and loving every minute of it.

By June 1947, he was reassigned again to St. Joan of Arc in St. Clair Shores. At this time, he almost faced death. He had a small kidney stone, and complications developed from its removal, but he pulled through.

In March 1953, the chancellor, Fr. Bud Kearns, called him to the chancery. Cardinal Mooney wanted him to become the administrator of Our Lady of Victory Mission. He was told it was an all-black parish on West Eight Mile and Washburn in Detroit. He was walking on air to get his first parish after being ordained only fourteen years. He was also told that he was not expected to stay there very long. "You're just an administrator for a mission church."

Before Fr. DeCneudt left, he came to love this church and its people. He benefited from the foundation laid by the two previous priests, so by the time of his arrival, the school was on the verge of opening its doors for the first time. "I spent more mornings in that boiler room than I care to remember, trying to control the heating bill through the tough winters." He officiated at the ground-breaking ceremony on February 21, 1954, and the laying of the cornerstone ceremony on June 20, 1954.

He performed a lot of baptisms and marriages during his assignment, and Catholic family life was firmly established. Sometimes he visited the classrooms, and the children would stand up and say, "Good morning, Father, God Bless you, Father!" If a parent came to visit, the class would greet him or her the same way. DeCneudt stayed for six years and then had to leave for a new assignment.

Fr. DeCneudt was assigned to the Church of the Madonna by 1959. It was located on Oakman Boulevard and Twelfth Street. This is where the children went while OLV school was under construction. Madonna was becoming predominantly black at the time of Father's arrival. It had a strong nucleus of whites that he had to ask to learn how to share. His years at Our Lady of Victory had been a great help to him for the challenges that lay ahead. He started an adult sponsor program for newly admitted converts into the church. It was an exciting five years and six months.

In January 1964, Archbishop Dearden asked him to accept an appointment to become the pastor of Our Lady Queen of All Saints in Fraser. He was uprooted again. The parish had just experienced the sudden death of its priest, Fr. Joseph Szymaszek. While serving there, Fr. DeCneudt became a monsignor on October 3, 1965. He retired eighteen years from the date of his assignment in Fraser.

He managed to go back to Belgium in June 1971 with his two sisters to see his native land. It had been thirty-four years since he had been there.

Then in December 1971, he was rushed to St. John's hospital with what the doctor called an acute coronary. He was hospitalized for several weeks and recuperated in Phoenix, Arizona.

One of the results of Vatican II was the need to establish in each parish a parish council. Monsignor DeCneudt had to learn how to get one started and then learn how to live with one. It was a time of trial and error, and he had to learn the difference between delegation and abdication. Something that is easy enough on paper but difficult in practice.

On June 21, 1981, while getting ready for bed, he experienced a sudden pain in the right leg. The doctors diagnosed it as an aneurysm. After three or four operations in the next forty-eight hours, the doctor told him the leg had to come off. He adjusted over time to his prosthesis and weathered some additional health crises along the way.

While he was away from Our Lady of Victory all those years, some of the members still maintained a relationship with the monsignor, including his former housekeeper, Mary Elizabeth Robinson. He made a positive impact that will never be forgotten.

Those who knew him had the impression that Monsignor DeCneudt clearly enjoyed being a priest and had the rare opportunity to see how other ethnic groups live in the process. He forged strong bonds with some of the OLV members and that puts him in a class with Fr. Alvin Deem and Fr. Hubert Roberge.

The Rosa-Green Family

Arthur and Ruth Rosa-Green II were among the early pioneers of OLV. Ruth was an accomplished poet, author, and teacher. She wrote several books, and at various times you could find one of her poems in the parish bulletin. She and her husband, Arthur, raised three daughters, Angela, Carol, and Irma, and one son, Arthur III.

Ruth's parents, Antonio and Mary Gillem Rosa, were among the early pioneering families who developed the West Eight Mile Road area from Greenlawn to Birwood. Mary celebrated her 103rd birthday in 1990 with family and friends.[24] She lived over two decades longer than Antonio, who passed away in 1966.

When Ruth returned to Michigan in 1945, she learned about OLV Mission. Having embraced Catholicism during her junior year in college, she was delighted to be able to attend a church near her home. She and her father, Antonio Rosa, and daughter Angela attended mass at Our Lady of Victory and participated in the many activities and programs, along with other early members, until the church was built.[25]

According to Smith, to attend Catholic service before 1943, blacks had to travel into the city parishes in the archdiocese. Black Catholics had two parishes set aside for them, similar to the other ethnic parishes: St. Peter Claver, relocated at Sacred Heart in 1938, on the near east side of downtown Detroit, and St. Benedict the Moor served blacks on the west side. Ruth recalled traveling with her father, an Italian, on the trolley to St. Peter Claver for services during the 1920s.

The Birdhurst Center, by Ruth's childhood recollection, was constructed around 1925. Birdhurst was originally built as a rural school building. By 1944, the center was showing movies every Friday night at 6:30 PM with an admission price of sixteen cents. Doc Washington co-owned a drugstore near

Bethlawn and West Eight Mile Road. She remembers also that he owned a black baseball team called the Eagles.

The public school drop-out rate was problematic, because the children were alienated from education by racial discrimination. They were steered away from college prep courses and were forced to regard themselves as potential laborers. By 1944, the North-Western Mothers Club, which was a group of concerned black parents, voiced its concerns about the school problem. The children in Royal Oak Township living west of Wyoming left their neighborhood to attend secondary schools. They were bused to Northern High School in Detroit from across Eight Mile, because the nearby white school, Oak Park in Oakland County, would not take them.

By 1945, the population growth of the western section of the township required that a new elementary school be built. That year the children of the area entered the new George Washington Carver elementary with a new teacher from Wilberforce University, Ruth Rosa-Green. In 1947, Sarah Jane McKenzie-Hilton joined Ruth at the new school.[26]

The Rosa-Green family spans five generations. Arthur Green II passed away much too soon. Ruth took the name Leonard when she married Washington Leonard, another important member of the parish community, in October of 1991. She is a member of Presentation—Our Lady of Victory Church and belongs to the KPC Ladies Auxiliary Claver Court #189.

Fred and Almeta Carruth

A Personal Account by Almeta (Dolly) Carruth-White

If you ever want to know what really happened as far as history goes, it's best to start with someone who has lived it, if you are fortunate enough to find such an individual. Fred and Almeta Carruth played such an important and prominent role in Our Lady of Victory's early years that it cannot be stressed enough how much that point was brought home by their daughter, Almeta White. They would have been completely overlooked were it not for Gloria Cook, who told me about Almeta's family and their importance to this story. An interview took place on October 30, 2002. All the parishioners knew Almeta by the nickname "Dolly," so that is how I have referred to her throughout this book.

Dolly's account of events paints a poignant and stressful environment for a young black girl growing up in Detroit in the forties. Some of the memories were good, and some not so good, but Dolly has a way of telling even the bad times with humor, and that is a rare gift.

At the time that Our Lady of Victory was founded, the Carruth family was attending Holy Ghost Church, which was set aside for the blacks on the northeast side of Detroit in an area known as Conant Gardens. They moved to the projects of Royal Oak Township in the summer of 1945 and used to take the Conant bus over to Holy Ghost to attend Sunday services, because they didn't know that OLV existed. When they did become aware of the church, they started attending. Dolly recalls that the church started with Anna Bates, probably in her home. The first meetings were held with Fr. Alvin Deem. When her family arrived, the church was moving into a makeshift building, which later became a drugstore on Eight Mile and Cherrylawn.

Fr. Alvin traveled from Duns Scotus to do the service, and OLV was so close to having their own building when apparently, the lease ran out. That's when they moved to the Birdhurst Recreation Center. They used the lower floor for services. The members would set up the chairs for Sunday Mass and then take them down. It seemed to Dolly that Fr. Alvin Deem had moved on by that time, because he was a missionary and that was his commission, and Fr. Roberge had already come to be the new pastor.

Dolly discovered as an adult that the church building came from St. Juliana. They moved it from the east side over to West Eight Mile and Washburn, put it on top of the foundation, and that was OLV. This church was home to her and her parents for a long time. There is an official copy of a deed in the archives along with a letter of donation made by St. Juliana, which the archdiocese turned over to Our Lady of Victory.

Fred Carruth was very active in the life of the parish. He was one of several committee men who certified annual reports and historical data. Five members were appointed each year by the cardinal. The committee men acted as advisers to the pastor concerning improvements and expansion of the parish and examined the parish reports for the chancery. There was no parish council at this time as in most parishes.

The Committee Men

Edward Cardinal Mooney	John Cardinal Dearden
February 18, 1951	February 14, 1965
Eaton Metoyer	Washington Leonard
Clarence Jordan	Willie Bouie
Josef Baker	Alfred Cook
Lawson Conway	Joseph R. Flowers
Antwon Baker	Fred Carruth

Fred Carruth was the grand knight of the Knights of St. Peter Claver, Santa Maria Council #105. His wife, Almeta, was active in her own right. She belonged to the ladies auxiliary and was president of the Oblate Sisters of Providence Guild. And as was mentioned earlier, she organized the members to keep the nuns' garments clean. The Carruths did so many wonderful and necessary activities to keep the parish going and set a fine example for their daughter in the process.

Almeta "Dolly" White Graduation

Dolly attended Sacred Heart School near downtown Detroit, because OLV did not have a school at that time. She describes vividly how she and other classmates left their homes at seven o'clock in the morning in order to arrive at Sacred Heart in time for eight o'clock mass taking a bus and two streetcars.

"The Conant bus ran up and down Eight Mile Road. You took the Conant bus to the Fairgrounds, and then you boarded the Woodward streetcar down to Manchester in Highland Park. You walked two blocks and boarded the Oakland Street car, and that took you down to Beaubien and Eliot. You got off and walked three blocks to Sacred Heart."

Dolly belonged to Sacred Heart's choir. Each grade had a Sunday that they were assigned to sing the Mass. Because Dolly's home parish was OLV, and she was attending school at Sacred Heart because there was no school at OLV, she had to bring a letter from Fr. Roberge to her teacher at Sacred Heart, proving that she went to Mass at OLV. This had to be quite confusing and stressful to a very young person.

Transportation appeared to be very efficient in those days, but Dolly, in a thoughtful moment, said, "There was a price to be paid for having to go so far to school." At the time, she and her friends were too young to understand the ramifications of what they had to do to get a good education and to belong to a Catholic Church in the forties.

Dolly sums up Sacred Heart Church history:

> Sacred Heart is referred to as the mother church of the blacks in the city of Detroit. In 1930, it was originally a German church. In reference to the historic old St. Mary's downtown, the German people that lived uptown felt that it was too far for their children to walk to school, especially in the wintertime, so they built Sacred Heart simply because in those days you had to have a church before you could have a school. It was built in 1875, and then they built the school in 1889. Now in 1933, the area had changed. Colored people started worshipping in the schoolroom of Old St. Mary's downtown. They eventually moved uptown to what is now St. Peter Claver. That church is still there at the corner of Eliot and Beaubien Streets. It is a Headstart program now, but the activity center building across the street is still there. And when the German people realized that their congregation had dwindled, the diocese gave Sacred Heart (the building) to the colored people, and they had a procession right down Eliot Street from Beaubien and Eliot down the street to Rivard and Eliot in 1933.
>
> The priests that were assigned to Sacred Heart were not diocesan priests. They were the Holy Ghost Fathers. They set up Holy Family in Inkster, Holy Ghost in Conant Gardens, and St. Benedict the Moor on the west side, which is now a non-Catholic church. But those were the churches that served the colored people in the city of Detroit.

And then she said, "OLV was dedicated to what was called *missa recitata*" [reciting the mass].

"We had to learn all that Latin, so that when Father chanted, '*Dominus vobiscum* [The Lord be with you],' we knew every response. That's one reason why we learned our Latin so well."

When OLV School was finally built, the children attending began learning their Latin and singing in the choir, which was the way it was in Catholic churches in the city of Detroit in the forties and fifties.

The subject of evangelization really got to Dolly. To this day, she still does not understand the archdiocese's evangelization efforts. Here is what she had to say:

The nuns came in 1948, but they evangelized from the time they arrived. When all four of the nuns couldn't go, two of them would team up with two lay people. The school was not built. They went from house to house knocking on doors, telling people that Our Lady of Victory was going to have a school, and that in order for their children to attend, they must be members of the church. That's how they evangelized! People joined because they wanted their children to go to Catholic schools. It was phenomenal! And, of course, they had those big bonnets, which were attention getters and a big hit in the black community.

Dolly said that "the first four nuns that came were Mother Providencia (she left the order since then), Sr. Mary of Nazareth (she's Sr. Thelma now), Sr. Mary Patricia (deceased), and Sr. Mary Augustine, who is still living at Holy Name of Mary Parish in Chicago." Dolly has stayed in touch with her over the years.

Another issue that bothered Dolly was that she could not understand why Our Lady of Victory was labeled a mission church.

Archdiocesan priests staffed Our Lady of Victory. But the Holy Ghost Fathers staffed Holy Ghost, Sacred Heart, Holy Family, St. Benedict the Moor, and old St. Mary's downtown. And it made a difference. You are under the Archdiocese of Detroit. And that's why I didn't understand the label "Our Lady of Victory Mission," because the Holy Ghost Fathers were missionary priests, and their primary work was always among the Indian and Negro missions. We used to collect for them once a month. But Our Lady of Victory was not staffed by missionary priests after Fr. Alvin Deem left.

So OLV was functioning as a mission, with the missionary priest gone and an Archdiocesan priest in his place. Perhaps another reason (though not a good one) to call it a mission had to do with the fact that there was extensive evangelization going on. There were no so-called "cradle Catholics" in large numbers in the black church. Fr. Hubert Roberge was a priest ahead of his time. He was a real disciple of Christ ... one of the few who understood the plight of the blacks, not only in the church, but also in society as a whole.

Being a chaplain at Immaculata High School gave Fr. Roberge an opportunity to get black girls into the school. Dolly arrived in 1952 along with Yvonne Wilson. Alta Sears came later. Others like Jean Smith, Sandra Session, and Genevieve Oldham went to Our Lady of Mercy because of Fr. Roberge's help. All were from Our Lady of Victory.

Fr. Roberge was not a missionary priest. He was a rare find for archdiocesan personnel. That is what was so brilliant and so timely about his historic assignment, which was very fortunate for Our Lady of Victory. It was a smart move by the archdiocese, but they didn't take it to the final step—making Fr. Roberge a permanent pastor. Even after he left, the parishioners kept up with him, and he kept up with them. He loved Our Lady of Victory. When he got sick, Dolly's parents dropped everything and went to see him wherever he was.

✝

Dolly remembers the housekeepers, James and Margaret Evans, and their children. They lived in a house behind the convent. There were maintenance quarters for the janitorial staff. The house looked like a little garage, and James served as janitor and choir director. The Evanses had thirteen children, and they outgrew the house quickly. He was eventually hired by the State of Michigan and worked at a corrections facility out in Plymouth, and the family moved on in life.

Dolly belonged to the first teenage choir at OLV. The members included Beth Wilson, Betty Honeycut, and her sister Barbara Ann, Alice Hinds, Ed Wilson, Teddy Horn, and Sr. Sharon's brother Stanley Young.

"It took three of us to do the solo lines to 'Panis Angelicus.' We couldn't remember it! One could remember the words, the other had the best voice, and the other could remember the music. Evans taught us after Sr. Patricia moved on. He is still with Norah Duncan's Choir."

Norah Duncan IV was appointed Blessed Sacrament Cathedral's music director and organist in 1980 by the late John Cardinal Dearden, and he gained national prominence over the years with his works.

Dolly recalls a large family that lived in her neighborhood—the Lairds, which included Alta Sears, Thelma, Robert, and Linwood. Both brothers are now deceased. These are the siblings that she grew up with. They belong to St. Cecilia parish today.

She talked about the Clothilde Smith Family—Richard E., Joseph, and Jean. Then the DuPlessis family came up, which includes Marlene Talley, Veronica Cunningham, and daughter Karen Cook, daughter-in-law of Alfred and Gloria Cook. Karen sings with the Metro Gospel Choir.

The pillars of the church were Ed Wilson Sr. and Ella Mae. They had three children: Yvonne, Edward, and Judith. They lived in Royal Oak Township. Mr. Wilson worked at the post office.

The Rankins were another large family, and William was the oldest. Dolly knew him as Billy. One of the daughters, Angela, babysat for her. There were ten siblings.

The Carruth family members are Fred, Almeta, and Almeta White, their only daughter. Almeta died in 1980, and Fred married Virginia Douglass. Fred died in 1983, and Virginia died in 2002.

✝

There was an ugly side to growing up black and Catholic. There was the unspoken race problem. This research has helped to reveal the dynamics that make up the Catholic Church and how those dynamics fueled discrimination. The diocese had what seemed like churches on every corner. One for the Irish, one for the Germans, one for the Poles, etc., because these groups did not want to mix. Dolly's instructor talked about this very issue in a church history class. She said, "In the 1900s, the church was run by the Irish, but every group was fighting against each other. Blacks were at the bottom of the barrel."

Discussion turned to the infamous "wall." There have been many wild rumors out there about the wall, so it was exciting to get the real story.

> The wall was real! When World War II ended, people bought homes up to Pinehurst Street and anything west of that wall. Blacks were putting up $500 deposits, an exorbitant sum of money to move into those homes. [It was the price they had to pay to get decent housing which most could not afford. It served as a deterrent to control the numbers. The wall stopped the flow completely.]
>
> On the east side of the wall was Birwood Street, the projects, and the Quonset huts, which were army barrack-type structures or jerry-built housing that the government built to house blacks coming up north in the forties for jobs in the auto industry. They ran the wall right in back of the alley on Birwood Street to separate the blacks from the whites. The private homes started on the west side of the wall. That's where Pinehurst and Monte Vista streets were located, right near Presentation Church.

West of the wall was home to some of the most beautiful housing structures in the city. And the housing codes were strictly enforced. The difference between the east and west side of that wall was like night and day.

Those rumors about the wall spawned a legendary following over the years that fueled the debate of whether the story was fact or urban legend. And now the myth can finally be explored. Every one of the early pioneers has stories of how racism affected black Catholics and how they coped with it personally.

Dolly talked about her mother, Almeta, working for a family named McGrail, who lived on Pinehurst near Presentation Church during the period from 1948 to 1950. The McGrails asked Almeta to come to work one Saturday, which was out of the ordinary because she did not work on Saturdays. She realized that she would be unable to get to Our Lady of Victory in time for Saturday afternoon confession, so she stopped at Presentation Church.

The priest heard her confession and at the end of it he asked, "Are you a member of this church?"

"No."

"Which parish do you belong to?"

"Our Lady of Victory."

"I suggest that you go there in the future for your confessions."

Dolly said, "Mother was shocked and discussed her experience with some of the other church members."

On another occasion, Almeta was admitted to Mt. Carmel Hospital. The hospital put her in a private room although she knew her insurance would not cover such a luxury. One of the parishioners, whose name was Freddie, worked in housekeeping at the time and just happened to come around the corner and saw that the room was occupied.

Freddie looked in and said, "Mrs. Carruth, they put you in this room? A man just died in here two hours ago."

Mother wanted to know why they put her in that room that quickly. The administrator of the hospital came to talk to her and said, "Well, you wouldn't want to be in a room with white women, would you?"

She said, "That's all my insurance could afford."

She decided to discharge herself and went down to old St. Mary's Hospital downtown, which ultimately became Detroit Memorial.

Jim Crow segregation might have been subtler in parochial schools, but the archdiocese did keep children separate in those schools. When she was a child, Dolly's family was living on the west side of Detroit on a street called Firwood, which placed them in St. Dominic Parish. Her mother wanted to send

Dolly to the school. The priest asked, "Wouldn't she be happier with her own kind?"

These incidences were insulting and illuminate the racial intolerance that was allowed to fester in the diocese. The priests perpetrating the racist acts never thought that they were doing anything wrong, so the offenses were never dealt with.

Where were black Catholics to go? Like their white brethren, they sought refuge from life's problems in the church. Unfortunately, too often it not only failed to offer sheltering arms but actually shunned them. This is a church that prides itself on its diversity, but has shown its reluctance to grapple with the problems associated with that diversity.

Dolly is very active in the Claver organization at Sacred Heart where she is still a member. It is called the Knights of Peter Claver Ladies Auxiliary, St. Anne Court #71. The men belong to the Knights of St. Peter Claver Fr. Kapp Council #71.

She has been an officer of the Michigan Central Committee for a number of years and attends all meetings and conferences locally and nationally. She has been a grand lady in her court. She lives her faith through action. Fred and Almeta would be very proud of their daughter's commitment today, because she is carrying on the work that they started at Our Lady of Victory Church.

The Claude Carter Family

By Marcella Carter and Ona Carter-Harris

Doing this interview was a rare opportunity, as there was no other information on the Carter family of pioneers. Their story is both informative and fascinating. The meeting took place on May 18, 2005, at 10:00 AM at Ona Harris's home.

There were four children in the family of Claude and Marcella Carter: Ona, Clarence Michael, Claudia, and Sharon. They were among the first families to be baptized by Fr. Alvin Deem. Marcella recalls how the family came to Detroit and to the church.

I am from Longview, Texas. I met Claude in 1942 while visiting my father. I got a job and decided to stay. My father already knew Claude, and I was up here a little over a year when we got married. Claude is from Kansas City. He came up to visit a sister, and she got him a job, and he stayed. Another sister came up, and they all got jobs and stayed in Michigan. We lived down on Jay Street on the south end of Detroit.

After we got married, we settled in the northwest area. We were Baptist initially. My daddy's wife was affiliated with Catholics, and we started going to Catholic functions and socials, and I liked the education and how they took time with the children. Other schools were not like Catholic schools, and that is what drew us to the faith. Claude went into business for himself selling coal and ice. In the winter, he sold ice and coal; in the summer, he sold ice. We moved in the [West Eight Mile] area where he also started a landscaping business.

There was a friend (I don't remember his name) going to Presentation. He and Claude got together, and they started Our Lady of Victory with Fr. Alvin. My husband met him when we were going to the functions. We joined and my husband knew so much about the Bible that Father Alvin let him give instructions along with Mother Bates. John Luckett, another member, also gave instructions.

When the move was made [to the new church], it was just a crowd going in. Father Alvin was talking to the congregation about where we had come from up to the present. He was in Our Lady of Victory before he was sent away. He was crazy about that church and was a little disappointed that he had to leave.

Initially, Ona started kindergarten at St. James School. She was only six years old when she had to board the bus every day to get to the school, which was located in Ferndale on Woodward near Nine Mile Road. She got on that bus every day by herself. Then the Carter children started going to Madonna and St. Paul and were put back a grade just to get in. Ona repeated second grade. They put Claudia back in kindergarten.

"Can you imagine that? How can you put someone back in kindergarten? They put everybody back! In spite of what happened, everybody that had to repeat a grade seems to be very successful today. Most of us did very well to have been dealt this injustice. We were not dumb. It was just their mentality. It had nothing to do with racism. My father used to say it all the time that white people used psychology to keep the blacks back, and now we are doing it to ourselves."

The Carter children started going to Presentation and were the first blacks admitted. Ona started in the third grade and graduated in 1958. The rest of the siblings graduated at Presentation as well. The Carters took no particular pride in blazing this trail; they did what they had to do to get a good education for their children. But OLV was not built yet, and Claude wanted his children together in a Catholic school close by. All the years that the children were attending Presentation, Ona recalled that the students didn't treat them any differently, and they never encountered any racism.

Claude Carter was the type of individual who understood business and how to save money, and so he instituted most of the fundraising events at OLV in its early beginnings. He was an innovative businessperson way ahead of his time. He sold Christmas trees at Christmastime. Private vendors had never sold trees, yet Claude reasoned, "Everybody needs a Christmas tree, and why not take them up there and sell them?"

The family set the holes and placed the trees on the Washburn Street side of the church where they were displayed and sold. The trees could be seen from West Eight Mile Road. "That was the first time anyone had ever seen trees sold like that," said Ona, "except at Franks Nursery, a popular nursery and crafts store in the area."

Ona talked about the talent shows her father put on with the involvement of the nuns. He organized pancake breakfasts once a month and spaghetti dinners often to raise money. The Feather Party was implemented around this time and was held every year. The Feather Party coincided with the Thanksgiving holiday season and raised money for the church. First prize was a big basket filled with a turkey and food items for some lucky family. Everyone played Bingo and sometimes the church sponsored auctions. It was a very successful, annual event.

Claude worked with St. Vincent DePaul along with Washington Leonard. After the members made the move to the new location, Claude became the religious education instructor. He was instrumental in starting Our Lady of Victory Federal Credit Union. Hattie Braddock ran it, and Claude, John Luckett, Tom Lester, and Fred Carruth were the first board of directors. Claude had something to do with the school, too. He was a key player in every aspect of parish family life. He would go and see the cardinal all the time, and a lot of those visits had to do with incidences of racism. He wouldn't bite his tongue.

The fact that he had to go and see the cardinal at all was problematic. It would be difficult to pinpoint one single thing that defined racism, because it was everywhere; and so one can assume that Claude was just more vocal than most in his style of addressing it. His answer was simply to go to the source.

Ona emotionally relives the church closing, and she goes on to talk about her family's affiliations in the various organizations at Our Lady of Victory:

> The biggest mistake ... biggest racist act of the Catholic Church was when they engineered the merger. Our Lady of Victory was self-sufficient, always had been. We used to have talent shows, and Mrs. Bouie practically stayed up there cooking for all the fundraising events that went on. She would go over to the rectory sometimes to help, and Mr. Bouie handled the church plant.
>
> My father was a member of the Knights of St. Peter Claver, and I and other children attended sodality meetings every Saturday in the convent.

There were little projects, and the theme was the Blessed Mother. There was the Ladies Auxiliary but no junior division of the Claver Organization. It was just the Sodality Girls, which was the equivalent of the Junior Daughters division at that time.

OLV was very self-sufficient. One of the key reasons it did not succeed was because people got discouraged with the parade of priests that came and went.

When you consider how there were seven priests in and out of Our Lady of Victory from the period of 1943 through the merger compared to two priests assigned to Presentation from 1941 through the merger, it's easy to see how members could become very discouraged and frustrated. To date, twenty priests have served as administrators (See Appendix).

Marcella recalls that after the church was established, Fr. Alvin was there for what seems like only a second, and then he was gone. When Fr. Roberge arrived, his sister came and lived in the rectory with him. She kept house and cooked for him up until he left.

Then there was one incidence when thugs broke into the sacristy. Fr. DeCneudt called Claude and told him that someone had broken in and made a big mess. Claude reassured him that he would take care of it, and he did.

Being an archdiocesan priest and Belgian, Fr. DeCneudt had little opportunity to be knowledgeable about the needs of a different ethnic group. He was fortunate to have Claude there to help him acclimate to ministering to an all-black parish. Claude's presence had to have been a great comfort to the new priest who had to forge his own path.

The first maintenance workers at the church according to Ona were her Uncle Tommie Carter and his wife Aunt Tommie Lou (her mother's sister). They lived in the little garage house behind the church off from the road next to the alley. They had two children, Jennifer and Naverra. Tommie worked on the grounds and did janitorial work and anything else the nuns needed. The nuns were there before the school was built. The Tommie Carter family stayed in that little house until just before the fifties, and then they moved on.

All of the Carters lived in the area. The Claude Carter family was the third black family living in the area on Monte Vista Street in 1949. The Bouie's lived right next door to them. Then suddenly, Claude was dead of a heart attack in 1981, just before OLV officially closed its doors for the last time.

Ona Carter Harris is active in the Church of the Precious Blood, located in Detroit. She belongs to the Knights of St. Peter Claver, Most Precious Blood

Court #307 and is the junior daughter counselor. Precious Blood merged with St. Francis de Sales in Detroit in November 2005. The new name is St. Peter Claver Catholic Community.

Claude, Marcella, and Ona in 1943. *Photo supplied by Ona Harris.*

The Pioneering Spirit Continues

The DuPlessis-Ward family was part of Our Lady of Victory's early years. The parents, Emil Joseph Sr. and Delores, can trace their Catholic roots to New Orleans, Louisiana. Emil Sr. died while the children were still young, and Delores married William Ward. Some of the siblings took the name Ward, and some did not. The DuPlessis children are Emil Joseph DuPlessis Jr., Florine DuPlessis-Anderson, Marlene Ward-Talley, and Veronica Ward-Cunningham.

Emil Jr. married Jean Smith, daughter of another pioneer family. The ceremony took place at OLV Church. They moved to New York for a while and then returned and settled in the Detroit area.[27] The church records list the baptism of their twins, Jeannette Yvonne and Jacqueline Marie, on October 8, 1961.

Marlene said that "Fr. Alvin always headed straight for the candy jar when he visited. He was quite a character." She got married in the church in 1956 by the Rev. Ferdinand DeCneudt. Three of her six children were baptized there.

Veronica married Donald Cunningham, who is now deceased. Their daughter Karen is married to Jeffrey Cook, son of Alfred and Gloria Cook.

The Smith Family includes the parents, Clothilde and Joseph Smith from Biloxi, Mississippi, and their children, Richard E., Joseph Jr., Marshall, Jean, and Melvin. The family played an important role in the early years of OLV and was very close to the pastor and the nuns.

According to Jean, her family lived on Washburn Street right next to the church, so their lives and all activities centered around the church. As mentioned, Jean became a DuPlessis through her marriage to Emil, Jr.

Richard did his research on the development of Our Lady of Victory and the West Eight Mile Community while attending Eastern Michigan University. His research helped in the development of Our Lady of Victory's complete story.

He and his siblings were living the history of Our Lady of Victory, so he must have been inspired to write about it. There aren't too many people who would attempt such a tremendous task.

✝

Betty White-Palmer is a member of the merged Presentation—Our Lady of Victory Church. Her roots go back to OLV's beginnings, starting with her parents, Icim and Edna White. Betty used to work at the Goodwill Supermarket on Wyoming and West Eight Mile Road in Royal Oak Township, right where a senior citizen's complex now stands, and she knew all the early members more by sight than name.

Betty has a history of firsts, starting with her family. She was the first of two girls out of a family of six siblings: Cicero (deceased), Icim Jr. (deceased), Eugene (deceased) Clifford, and Juanita. Her family was part of the first group to be baptized; and hers was the first class to receive Holy Communion in 1944. She was the first young person to crown the Blessed Mother at the first May crowning ceremony. She was dressed in white and wore a veil for the ceremony. The May Crowning was a ritual performed at all Catholic churches. The parishioners would form a line outside of church and walk around a block singing hymns and saying prayers, culminating with of the crowning of the statue of Mary. Usually a young girl was designated to crown the statue. Betty was also among the first group of young Sodalists. She provided a list which appears in the Appendix.

Betty recalls that her brother Eugene was part of the second or third class in the early years that made their first Holy Communion. There was no Catholic school to attend, so they all had taken religious instruction.[28]

Betty is a Lady of Grace of the Knights of St. Peter Claver, Ladies Auxiliary, Presentation—Our Lady of Victory Court #189 and she does catering for funerals and fundraising events. She extends her hospitality to Sr. Sharon Young whenever she comes to Detroit to see family and friends.

†

Washington Leonard and his wife Lillie (both deceased) came to Our Lady of Victory in 1949. Their youngest son, Leslie, attended and graduated from the school. There was a set of twins among his older children, Billy and Benny (one died in an auto accident); a daughter, Betty Leonard-Bradley, now deceased; and a son, Timothy. The older children had to attend other Catholic schools in the area.

In 1970, Washington was commissioned as a minister of service. He has served with each of our pastors since that time. His ministry included making home visits to the homebound, shut-ins, and visits to hospitalized members of the parish. He was on call at the parish center on weekdays to advise and counsel those who came to him. He worked closely with the Society of St. Vincent DePaul. He served at the Sunday Masses and at special functions. He assisted in training the apprentice ministers of service as well as being of service to the new priests.

He was a bridge between the many priests who ministered to the members over the years. He brought to the pastoral team a wealth of experience and knowledge of OLV and its people. He was a living connection to the tradition of Mother Anna Bates.[29]

It was a natural fit that two pillars of the church community would team up in matrimony. The wedding reception of Washington Leonard and Ruth Rosa-Green was held in the church social hall. It was a time of reminiscing among old pioneers and friends. It was a very beautiful ceremony. Washington Leonard was a tower of strength and stability in the parish community up until his death in 1995.

†

The following information on the McKenzie family comes from an interview between Richard E. Smith and Sarah Hilton for his college research in 1990.

Sarah Jane McKenzie-Hilton recalls that her father, Clarence McKenzie, had immigrated to the United States from Clarendon, Jamaica, with a ten-year stop in Havana, Cuba. The first American city where Clarence and his wife, Hepsiba Josephine, lived was Miami, Florida. However, after witnessing a lynching, Clarence and his wife moved in 1920 to Detroit. He was attracted to Detroit by the dream of obtaining employment at the Ford Motor Company.

Later near death, Clarence would tell his daughter that the job he so wanted would be the cause of his death. Clarence had been hired by Ford during the war. He worked at the River Rouge foundry and remained there until he was forced out with emphysema and died in 1966. He told his daughter Sarah Jane that he felt that his life had been a failure. Yet, he had provided for his family and sent three daughters to college—two of them later obtained master's degrees. Sarah received her degree from Wilberforce University in Ohio. Sarah Jane McKenzie-Hilton passed away on December 24, 2006.

The next piece is Sarah's memories written in her own words.

With the help of dedicated neighbors and potential parishioners, the mission was cleaned and renovated. Many generous benefactors donated monies and religious articles. Fr. Alvin Deem was young and energetic. He evangelized from door to door in the black Eight Mile Community. Madre Bates, a Catholic from birth, helped Fr. Alvin recruit members. She recruited my family. We were baptized and received our first Holy Communion on May 28, 1944. Combined, we were one of the largest families in the early days. The family included Hazel Louise McFadden (deceased), Josephine E. Chin (deceased), Clarice V. (deceased), Una Blanche, and Cousin Conrad C. Gordon.

Fr. Alvin taught the Catholic faith to potential parishioners and offered Mass on Sundays and holy days. During the summer months, with the help from the Sisters of Marygrove College, he held large religious programs at Birdhurst. He found help for the very poor. He helped youths to get in Catholic schools and encouraged them to go on for higher learning. Today many of those same youths are professional men and women contributing to society.

Shelton Johnson was the director of Birdhurst Community Center. He welcomed Fr. Alvin and parishioners to have Mass at Birdhurst since the membership was growing. Fr. Alvin later met Doc Washington, a tavern owner on Eight Mile Road in Ferndale, Michigan, who had an interest in the Eight Mile Road Community. He donated land to build Our Lady of Victory Church and school. Thomas Lester, a founder of the mission, plastered the new church. The parishioners were very excited to have the new Our Lady of Victory Mission.

The church grew, and it seemed like every three or six years the Archdiocese of Detroit would send a new priest to pastor Our Lady of Victory. Then in 1975, the archdiocese decided to close the church and school that the black Eight Mile Road Community had worked so hard to build. The parishioners were told to move over to the same Presentation church, which did not accept black families back in 1943. White families were moving from the area and OLV members were outraged. They felt betrayed that they had to give up the church and the school.

†

Foster Wilson Sr. and his wife, Earline, had a large presence in the growing new church. Foster came from Wilson, Louisiana, and Earline hailed from New Orleans. They were baptized at Our Lady of Victory in 1954 and became members of the Knights and Ladies of St. Peter Claver Council/Court. The senior Wilsons were the strength of the family and very much involved with the early church, including fund-raisers, and they were active in some of the numerous organizations. Their son, Foster Jr., was baptized after completing his training to be a minister of service in 1977. Foster and Earline are both deceased.

By 1975, Our Lady of Victory and Presentation had officially merged, although each still occupied separate buildings. After he became minister of service, Foster Jr. and his wife, Helen, became the grand knight and grand lady of the reestablished Our Lady of Victory—Presentation Council/Court #189. He subsequently left Our Lady of Victory and joined Precious Blood Church on Grove Street in Detroit.

He was a member of the Office of Black Catholic Affairs formerly known as the Black Secretariat. He was a liaison to Bishop Thomas Gumbleton and worked between the cardinal and the Office of Black Catholic Affairs. Because of his affiliation with this and a number of other important committees in the Catholic diocese, his leaving left Our Lady of Victory extremely vulnerable to the threat of closure.

Their children are Foster III, Lorna Thomas, Gregely, Kevin, and Elona. Lorna assisted in the expansion of the Junior Knights Division of Council #189 from the late 1980s up until around 1990. The entire family was very active and visible in the church for a number of years. Gregely practically lived in the office at Presentation—Our Lady of Victory after the merge. He was always there to greet all who came with a big smile.

Foster Wilson Jr. is a member of St. Peter Claver Catholic Community (formerly Precious Blood) and is a fourth degree knight of Precious Blood Council #307. Helen died in 1989. The family has since moved on with their lives.

✝

The proprietor of James H. Cole Home for Funerals serviced the members of Our Lady of Victory for years and always financed the raffle tickets for the annual parish festivals and every other event each year as well as financing both Presentation and Our Lady of Victory church calendars.

James H. Cole arrived at the time of the merger of the two churches. He was a fourth degree knight of St. Peter Claver. His ads were always featured in the parish bulletin, *The Good News.* He was a caring and warm individual, especially to bereaved parish families. His daughter, Karla, also became active in her father's business, often accompanying him for funeral services. They were a father and daughter team until his death. She runs the business now, but her father will always be remembered in our hearts.

An exhibit of pictorial narratives including the Cole family was displayed at the Skillman Branch Library in downtown Detroit near Cadillac Place People Mover Station from June through September 2005. It was a celebration of the untold story of Detroit's African American families.

✝

While not a member of Our Lady of Victory Church, Luther C. Keith played a major role in its beginnings. The Keith family includes his wife, Savella, and their children Gwendolyn, Luther Alton, Joyce, and Terrance. They were longtime members of St. Agnes Parish (name changed to Martyrs of Uganda). Luther's brother is the Honorable Judge Damon Keith, who forged his own legacy in the city of Detroit.

Keith was a real-estate agent, having inherited the business from his father. He helped Fr. Norman Dukette, the only black archdiocesan priest, procure the location for St. Benedict the Moor Church in a former Lutheran church building in 1927. Fr. Roberge requested that Keith's real-estate agency locate properties from time to time for the diocese. He was a prominent black Catholic who was well respected and connected in the Detroit Catholic community. He became an expert on Catholic affairs.

Keith organized the Knights of St. Peter Claver, Santa Maria Council #105 at OLV in 1949. He also worked with Msgr. Ferdinand DeCneudt on some community projects, including the Catholic Committee on Negro History, which he founded in 1955. Later it became the United Committee on Negro History. He was president from 1955 to 1966 and chairman until his death.

He was a community activist and a great role model for his children. He and his wife entertained mayors, Catholic Church leaders, and dignitaries from foreign countries in their home. They were the movers and shakers in the Detroit black community. Luther passed away on March 6, 1974. Savella passed on years later.[30]

✝

William Addison and Thelma Irene Rankin had one of the largest families at OLV. The children are William "Billy" A., Jerry L., Rita L. Willis, Angela Y. Rankin-Yohannes, Sharon D. Mitchell, Margaret L., David A., Cheryl T. Brown, Paula F. Heard, and Kevin P. Fr. Hubert Roberge baptized Billy at age three, Jerry at age two, and Rita at age one, together in the fall of 1950 shortly after the parents became members. The remaining younger seven siblings were all baptized as infants. Billy, a second-grader; Jerry, a first-grader; and Rita, a kindergartner, were among the first classes of students to attend Our Lady of Victory Catholic School when it opened in the fall of 1954. The boys joined the Altar Boys' Society, and all were trained under the guidance of Sr. Mary DePaul.

Interestingly, Thelma often filled in as a substitute teacher when the nuns were ill or away on business. The Rankin family was large, and the children were very active members for many years following their parent's example. They filled quite a few rows of seats in the church, and they are a very close-knit family. They have all moved away and left a real void in the church.[31]

✝

Sr. Mary Schutz was the founder of the Home Visitors of Mary, and she played a small role in the beginnings of Our Lady of Victory. Her name has come up in numerous of articles about OLV with no details on her life and who she was, so it seemed appropriate to present her connection to this history from materials she provided and a personal conversation.

Mary Schultz worked in a bookshop in the chancery building after she got out of college. While there, she decided to consider religious life. She had been working in the black community for eight to ten years. Josephine Van

Dyke Brownson was a math teacher at Cass Technical High School. She founded the Catholic Instruction League to catechize Catholic students attending Detroit's public schools and needed someone for one hour of catechism.

"I was taught to pass on what you got and had taught religious education at Lincoln school, so I volunteered to teach on Wednesdays," Mary said.

Once a year, Josephine would have a dinner for the teachers in appreciation for the work that they did. Mary was taking youngsters to St. Peter Claver, which moved to Sacred Heart, when she got a phone call from the Claver pastor that their teacher, Josephine, had been killed on Woodward Avenue in Detroit. Mary, Lou Murphy, and friends took over St. Peter Claver for a few years until it got crowded, sometime in the 1940s.

"While visiting families, I got the idea to go into religious life but couldn't find an order to go to. In searching for a religious community that would assure ministering to the black community, I consulted with Msgr. John Ryan, who had taken over religious education in the archdiocese from Josephine Brownson and now headed the Confraternity of Christian Doctrine."

Msgr. Ryan said, "Why not start a community that will go house-to-house inviting people to the church and also be responsible for catechetics?" He had personally known the Franciscan Sisters of the Atonement, who had worked in his home parish of Ogdensburg, New York, making house calls and teaching religion to public school children. Msgr. Ryan, on an assignment after ordination, visited every home within the boundaries of Blessed Sacrament parish. To prepare himself to "sell the parish" he enrolled in a Fuller Brush class, then among the most successful door-to-door salesmen.

Since Mary had worked at the Chancery Building Van Antwerp Library—now the Catholic Book Store—for ten years, and Cardinal Mooney did not hesitate to give permission to establish the new community, Msgr. Ryan asked that she test her intention. So for two years she did home visits as a layperson at St. Benedict the Moor, Our Lady of Victory, and Holy Ghost Parishes.[32]

Sr. Mary, who now resides with the Home Visitors of Mary on Boston Street in Detroit, explained that she could not remember what year she came to Our Lady of Victory, but she did not work with Mother Bates. Instead, she went house-to-house in the neighborhood under the direction of Msgr. Ryan. That would place the year some time between 1947 and 1949. She also remembers teaching religious education to the public school children at Our Lady of Victory during the 1950s.

1979 Photo © Dwight Cendrowski

May 5, 1963. Benefit Tea for Oblate Sisters of Providence.
Photo supplied by Doris West.

Fr. Alvin seated with First Communion Class of 1943 in front of storefront church.

First Anniversary of Knights of St. Peter Claver, Santa Maria Council #105. L to R: Leonard Proctor, James Gibson, Charles R. Smith, Joseph Glaser, and Fr. Roberge.

A very large first communion class photo taken during
Fr. Roberge's ministry.

Seated L to R: Sr. Virgine, Sr. Teresita, Fr. Roberge, and Sr. DePaul.
Standing L to R: Parishioner Willa Dean Sumpter, June Bell, Catherine
Ball, and Sharon Anderson.

May 18, 1952. Crowning of Mary ceremony. Center: Betty White-Palmer, prefect. She was the first young lady to crown the Blessed Mother. She is pictured with Fr. Roberge, the Junior Sodality Girls, and the altar boys.

Sitting are Mother Stella Marie Harris and Fr. Ferdinand DeCneudt. Standing L to R: Sisters M. Teresita Thomas, M. DePaul Yancy, and M. Stephane Smith.

Senior Sodality presents the Oblate Sisters of Providence with a check.

March 3, 1951. Vocation Day exhibit in Catholic Central's gym.
Mother Mary Patricia talks to a potential candidate.

Viola Wilkins with L to R: Sisters M. Andrew, M. Duschesne, M. Marcia,
Mother M. Charlotte, and Sr. M. Bridget.

February 21, 1954. Father DeCneudt and Mother Providencia
at ground-breaking ceremony for new school.

The monsignor is retired but still active today.

December 8, 1953. Fr. DeCneudt gives communion to Junior Sodality Girls. They turn out in those floppy white tams and powder blue capes.

October 3, 1954. Grand Knight Fred Carruth presents Fr. DeCneudt with a $500 check for school. First on left is the author's godfather, Thomas Cunningham.

Washington Leonard became the most important and loved patriarch of Our Lady of Victory church.

1949. Betty Palmer crowning the statue of Mary.

May Procession in the early 1950s. On the extreme right is Jean Smith-DuPlessis. In background is Cunningham's Drugstore in Royal Oak Township business district, just north of West Eight Mile Road.

L to R: Sr. Cyprian Jones, Mother M. Patricia Ford, Mayor Jerome Cavanaugh, Sr. Virginie Fish, and Savella Keith. *Photo supplied by Luther A. Keith.*

Sources

1. "Historical Data Section of the Annual Report." Our Lady of Victory Archives. 1945. Detroit.

2. Philip M. Fortier, Interview, University of Detroit Mercy. 8 September 2004.

3. *Afro-American and Catholic: The Second Generation of Mission Churches,* comp. and ed., Institute for Continuing Education (Detroit: Archdiocese of Detroit, 1975), 30.

4. Alvin Deem to Msgr. John C. Ryan, 16 March 1945. Archdiocese of Detroit Archives.

5. Gagnon, Fr. Joseph. *The Golden Jubilee of Fr. Alvin Deem,* OFM. comp. and ed. Jacqueline Majors & Sarah McKenzie-Hilton. 21 October 1990.

6. Franciscan Archives Cincinnati, Province of St. John Baptist. 10 January 2004.

7. John C. Ryan to His Eminence Edward Cardinal Mooney, 6 February 1946. Archdiocese of Detroit Archives.

8. Alvin Deem to Msgr. John C. Ryan. 30 September 1946. Archdiocese of Detroit Archives.

9. John C. Ryan to Very Rev. Romauld Mollaun, OFM 9 October 1946. Archdiocese of Detroit Archives.

10. Rev. Herbert Klosterkemper to Rev. Edward Hickey. 12 October 1946. Archdiocese of Detroit Archives.

11. Chancellor to Rev. Herbert Klosterkemper. 18 October 1946. Archdiocese of Detroit Archives.

12. Anne Purvis, Fax to the author. 3 April 2004.

13. Leslie Woodcock Tentler, *Seasons of Grace: The Diocesan Clergy.* (Wayne State University Press: Detroit, Michigan, 1994), 393.

14. Rev. Thomas Ebong to the author. November 2004.

15. Leslie Woodcock Tentler, *Seasons of Grace: Catholics in a Changing World.* 509.

16. Oblate Sisters of Providence Archives. Baltimore, MD.

17. Desiree Cooper, ed., "Lessons in Spirit," *The Detroit Free Press.* 22 March 2005, 1B.

18. Kathleen Cox, Telephone Interview. Marygrove College. 8 December 2003.

19. Sr. Wilhelmina M. Lancaster, *150th Anniversary, Oblate Sisters of Providence: Our Foundress.* 14 Feb. 1978.

20. George M. Anderson, ed. and comp. *Mother Mary Lange: Relying on Providence.* New York, America, 11 Oct, 2004, 22–23.

21. John C. Ryan to Rev. John A. Donovan. 21 July, 1948. Archdiocese of Detroit Archives.

22. *Afro-American and Catholic: Men and Women Religious*, comp. and ed., Institute for Continuing Education (Detroit: Archdiocese of Detroit, 1975), 35–36.

23. Sr. Elizabeth Harris. Comp. *Black Catholic Religious Commitment: Sr. M. Sharon Young, O.S.P..* (Archdiocese of Detroit, 1981).

24. Rebecca Beach ed. "A Happy 103rd to 8 Mile Settler." *Detroit Free Press.* 25 April 1990, 4B.

25. Ruth Rosa Green, ed. "A Church Closes, A Spirit Continues." 1 August 1982. Unpublished booklet.

26. Richard E. Smith, "Development of Our Lady of Victory and West Eight Mile." Unpublished research paper. Eastern Michigan University. 1990.

27. Home interview with Emil DuPlessis and Jean Smith. 21 September 2003.

28. Betty Palmer, Telephone and personal interview. 2004.

29. Parish Awards. comp. Presentation—Our Lady of Victory. 12 April 1990.

30. Luther A. Keith, "Tribute: A Black Man Discovers the Legacy His Father Bequeathed Him," *The Detroit News, Michigan,* 23, February 1986.

31. Jerry Rankin, e-mail. 26 August 2005.

32. Sr. Mary Schutz. *50th Anniversary Celebration: Beginnings Looking Back.* Home Visitors of Mary, Detroit. 21, November 1999.

III

The Catholic Community

Introduction

Part III introduces the Mission Church and the development of the West Eight Mile Community as told by some of the pioneers, including Richard E. Smith and Fr. Hubert Roberge, and the research efforts that went into the writing of this section. It is the story of a Catholic community in the making that never quite gets to the finish line. It follows the racist policies of the federal government that stifled the development of the black community and resulted in the building of the wall that neither blacks nor whites wanted. The story is about the construction of the church, rectory, and school, taken from OLV archives and treasured photographs.

There is a shortage of priests today throughout the region, but there has always been a shortage of black priests, and the subject is never open for discussion. Therefore, we probe into the question of why there are no black priests in significant numbers.

Nothing shapes a parish like its organizations, fund-raising, religious activities, and the various committees that run them. The members were innovative enough to start a credit union—the first and only one of its kind in a Catholic church. Our Lady of Victory had it all and still ended up becoming a forgotten statistic.

The Development of the West Eight Mile Community

October 3, 2006, would have marked the sixty-third anniversary of Our Lady of Victory if it were still in existence. This book is a tribute to a church that once stood proud among the residents in the West Eight Mile Community.

Richard E. Smith's research paper *Development of Our Lady of Victory and West Eight Mile* produced the following piece of history on the beginnings of the mission church and the development of the West Eight Mile Community.

Local entrepreneurs started their businesses in the emerging neighborhood supported by the residents. There was Jim Dolan's, a white-owned store; McCuller's Community Store; McCauley's Groceries and Meats (later becoming Steve's); Sheppard's, Lett's, and Worthy's. There was Charlie Rich's Pool Hall located at Greenlawn and West Eight Mile. It was owned by an Italian married to a black woman just like Antonio Rosa, one of the early pioneers of Royal Oak Township and the church. The Cockfield Funeral Home was servicing the area at the time. During the mid-1920s, the Atlantic and Pacific Tea Company (A&P) opened a store in the township. Sim's Gas Station and Variety store was located on the corner of West Eight Mile and Kentucky. The Fred Small Shoe Repair Shop was east of there on Eight Mile near Cherrylawn. On the north side at 8200 West Eight Mile was Uncle Tom's Bar-B-Q, operated by Thomas "Doc" Washington.

The owners of other black businesses lived in the community, such as Charles J. Wartman Jr., editor of the *Michigan Chronicle* newspaper. The black executives eventually organized The Merchant and Professional Association. The president of the association at the time was James Smith, owner of Smith Realty. Smith Realty was one of the first companies to sell homes west of Birwood in the Blackstone Park subdivision to blacks. The number of black merchants in the community was relatively high, especially since only 488 African-American-owned retail businesses operated in the entire state in 1929.

The outbreak of World War II urbanized the West Eight Mile Community. The population increased dramatically and bustled with the activity of thousands of recently migrated defense workers up from the South. A cement wall and restrictive policies governed the western and northern borders of the black community, while the southern border was bounded by a tract of undeveloped, city-owned land.

World War II converted industrial Detroit from building civilian automobiles and trucks to building military Jeeps and airplanes. This brought in an abundance of jobs, and blacks migrated to Detroit for the chance to work in Henry Ford's auto plant. Black men like Clarence McKenzie, who had earlier come to Detroit and failed to find work at Ford, found the doors open now and jobs waiting. Newcomers from the South like Eugene Smith and Washington Leonard found employment in defense plants, as well; however, after getting their jobs, the migrants had to find housing. Most newcomers did not have land, homes, or friends to help ease the housing situation, and they had little time to search. If they had family in the area, they would move in with them; if not, the workers rented sleeping quarters in the homes of blacks living in the city.

By the end of 1943, the housing situation in Detroit for blacks and their families was relieved somewhat with the construction of federal temporary housing. One of the sites selected by the federal government was the West Eight Mile Community. The temporary housing was supposed to alleviate the fears of a promise made to blacks, that they could build permanent homes someday soon. But the dream of building a modern home in the community had to wait for the war to end and for the policies of the United States Federal Housing Administration (FHA) to change. Land prices in the area rose dramatically during the war.

Archbishop Edward Cardinal Mooney had seriously entertained the thought of building a church and school in Royal Oak Township. On April 3, 1944, he approved the purchase of land and the building of a school located at Wyoming and Ithaca north of West Eight Mile Road.

By March 1945, it was evident that the representatives of the Public Housing Authority had been overconfident in their promises to permit the archdiocese to acquire property in the Oakdale Gardens subdivision. Originally estimated at $800, the price of the land grew to an appraised value of $8,000. The skyrocketing value of the land made the dream of acquiring property there all but impossible.

✝

While Smith's account certainly gives a historic picture of life in the developing community, Fr. Hubert Roberge paints a scene from his own perspective coming to the area in 1946. He was writing an article to run in the *Oblate News and Views*. It was sent in 1952 to a deceased Sister M. Helena, OSP, who was the editor of the now defunct publication. The article never ran because there is no record of it ever arriving, according to the Oblate Archives office.

Fr. Roberge records OLV's beginnings as it appears in the files. The church started in 1943 to serve the mile-square community adjacent to Eight Mile Road and Wyoming Avenue, and the area blossomed overnight with hundreds of wartime emergency housing units. He records eleven catechumens received into the church on May 27, 1944, and the largest mass baptism under Father Alvin on April 20, 1946, when forty-three new members were baptized into the faith.

Fr. Roberge describes how Fr. Alvin started the erection of an attractive church, seating 200, but by the time it was completed, Fr. Alvin was transferred. Fr. Roberge records how he, a priest of the Archdiocese of Detroit, was put in charge. There was the dedication of the new church in 1946 by the cardinal. He gives his perspective on the development of the new plant and the surrounding undeveloped land.

Fr. Roberge was dismayed at how undeveloped, dismal, and full of despair the area seemed. He compared life in the West Eight Mile Community to the missionary fields in Africa.

A year went by before a rectory was secured. The acquisition of land continued until enough property was acquired by the diocese to permit the future establishment of a complete parish plant. The holdup was a lease on the land held by the United States government while maintaining temporary war housing units on it; units that blacks and whites and the archdiocese wanted out of there. The lease was on a yearly basis with the right of renewal. The hope was that when the contract came up, Uncle Sam would decline to renew it, and that would free up the land for expansion.

During the period from 1943 to 1946, it was apparently difficult for the archdiocese to build a church and school and rectory in the West Eight Mile Community due to regressive government policies that sprang up as it tried to acquire the land needed to accomplish the complete revitalization and evangelization of the area. But according to Fr. Alvin Deem, it could have been accomplished in spite of these obstacles. The money was there, but the will was not.

In spite of these obstacles, the Oblate's arrival in 1948 started the real progress of building the school. The new church was complete, and the members had already settled in. While waiting for the day when a school would be operational, the nuns were busy principally with the instruction of adult women. They also taught catechism to the children attending public schools. They were responsible for organizing the Junior and Senior Sodality, the Girl Scouts, and various teenage social activities. Whenever a communion breakfast was held, the nuns were usually in charge. Directing adult study clubs; teaching the congregational singing and recitation of the Mass; instructing the altar boys; caring for the sanctuary and the altar linens; collecting merchandise and conducting rummage sales—these are just some of the activities listed when someone asks what the sisters did before there was a school. The school, however, was the goal so earnestly desired. Its realization would mark the era of abundant conversions. His Eminence Cardinal Mooney was ready to build as soon as Uncle Sam gave up his lease on the land. May of 1953 was the target date.[1]

The Wall of Shame

According to Smith, the Federal Housing Authority (FHA), which normally considered rising value an advantage in insuring home construction, looked down on the black community. New construction and its associated employment did not reach West Eight Mile Road. That would explain the undeveloped land and dismal look that Fr. Roberge described.

Smith said that the FHA, like the Home Owners Loan Corp. (HOLC), opposed the mixing of black and white in the same neighborhood, reasoning that property values in integrated neighborhoods would depreciate. Smith's description of the process used to justify this reasoning would be almost unbelievable or even laughable if it was fiction, but this is a real story.

To protect lenders' investments, FHA marked zones of development with grades that paralleled the colored borders used by the HOLC. The red lines, demarcating the areas of lowest ratings given by the HOLC, equated to the D zones the FHA used for black sections and older, impoverished white areas. Neither the red-lined nor D zones, nor the yellow or C zones, were areas in which FHA approved indemnified loans.

The developers were aware of the racial provisions of the FHA loans and tried covenants to protect their investment. In 1939, they added a racially exclusive covenant, yet Blackstone Park and Grand Park, mixed black and white neighborhoods still received negative FHA marks. Because both adjoining subdivisions were viewed as undesirable, a physical separation of the areas had to be made. The construction of a five-foot high cement wall, built by the developer along the alleyway of the western border appeased the FHA appraisers. Afterwards a re-evaluated walled area began receiving FHA approved loans for whites. The Wall, as early residents of the area called it, temporarily stopped the westward migration of the blacks. Its construction around 1941 created a deep resentment among the black residents. Though

115

they protested to the Detroit Housing Commission, their complaints were
fruitless, and the local monument to racism and segregation remained in place,
separating abutting backyards of black neighbors.

Sarah Hilton, in a discussion with Smith, recalled the wall and the anger it
created among the blacks that traveled to watch its construction. The edifice
of segregation was an aberration to blacks—there was no social contact with
the whites before its construction. It was to them unnecessary and a personal
affront.

The federal government had created social parameters that Smith describes
as an impediment that would hobble the black community. Blackstone Park,
with its wall and its racial covenants, was immunized from black encroach-
ment. On the black side of the wall, the FHA denied approval for home loans
and promoted the decay it believed generic to black neighborhoods. Here the
federal government built its temporary housing. The denial of loans not only
crippled the buying of homes by blacks, but it inhibited the expansion of
related black construction businesses. Black realtors and developers did not
have the property to show to black buyers, and black construction companies
were not able to fully participate in the building booms generated by the government guaranteed loans and the postwar economy.

The development of the area's war housing in the fall of 1943 was a tangled
web of social stratification and engineering. Both the established black residents and whites, who built the wall, resented the temporary housing. However, without access to the construction of FHA, and postwar Veteran
Administration (VA) loan indemnified housing, the recently migrated black
residents had no choice but to accept the temporary quarters.

The loan rejection was just part of a cycle of institutional racism. African
American people were limited in their access to the government-supported
housing in the city. Black occupancy in temporary housing was restricted to
government housing only in black neighborhoods, and black neighborhoods
were limited by covenants. The housing problems of the black southern-trans-
planted workers were enormous. The policies and practices of the City of
Detroit Public Housing Commission, and the pattern of incorporation practiced in Royal Oak Township, which directed the course of the community,
revealed a paradigm that resulted in the remains of the township being the
"unwanted black community."

The racial hostilities of Presentation parish west of the wall, and the rejection of black children from entry into the white parochial school was not an

issue to the Archdiocese of Detroit, because there was a distinct boundary to limit interaction—the wall.

✝

The wall was erected in the alley between Birwood and Mendota Streets. It stretched from the north at West Eight Mile Road, heading south to Pembroke Street. That's a three-block stretch of concrete to separate the races. Enforcement of housing codes was nonexistent on the black side of the wall. There were the Quonset huts, which were located on Wyoming, and they were not torn down until some time before the start of the new housing boom of the 1960s. Colonial-style modern brick homes with basements were constructed on Wyoming Street. Down another block, stood brick ranch homes with no basements alongside homes that had full basements and some leftover, very old housing stock that was never, to this day, torn down. Some of the streets were unpaved until the early 1960s. In spite of all this, the area started to improve after the new homes went up, and the neighborhood started to look clean and decent. The community was made up of black, two-parent, working families, wanting a better life.

Wyoming, a major artery, stretched north about three quarters of a mile into Royal Oak Township back south across West Eight Mile Road into Detroit for miles through the city. East of Wyoming in Detroit is an area of more uniform housing code, stretching all the way to Livernois Avenue, which used to be known as the beautiful Avenue of Fashion. It was called that because of the fashionable, upscale shops that lined the avenue, adhering to strict commercial codes. The 1967 riots destroyed this section, which stretched north of West Outer Drive to Louis the Hatter back south, midway past West Seven Mile Road anchored by B. Siegel's, a fashionable department store of the time. There was old housing stock in this area, but nothing compared to the lack of housing code enforcement from Wyoming to the wall behind Birwood.

On the east side of Wyoming in Royal Oak Township, were single-family homes, Ulysses S. Grant Elementary School, and Ferndale High School in the St. James Parish vicinity. If you lived on the east side, your children could attend the public high school and a few black Catholics went to St. James. West of Wyoming was the location of the one- and two-story housing projects with a few single-family homes sprinkled in the mix, most of them on Mendota Street.

The pattern of incorporation during the forties and fifties had whittled Royal Oak Township down to just a short stretch north past Northend Street, leading to a dense wooded area separating the black from the white residents living in the vicinity of West Nine Mile Road. Royal Township at one time stretched as far north as Troy, back south to West Eight Mile Road, and east to the Macomb County Line to Greenfield Road to the west. When white residents started to incorporate into their own cities, it reduced the township to the square mile tract of land it is today. Some time at the end of the 1950s going into the 1960s, Northend Street was zoned an industrial area, and the two-story projects in the township were soon torn down. New commercial businesses sprang up almost overnight.

There was George Washington Carver Elementary School but no high school on the west side that the teenagers could attend. So government funds was provided to bus those children to Northern High School in the Detroit Public School system, which was out of the township jurisdiction. This went on from the 1940s to the end of the 1950s.

Smith stated that housing to the west was a federal area and drew money from the national government to support its infrastructure. Money was given to the township to cover public safety. Carver was a federally subsidized project for those residents living in the government housing west of Wyoming. At the time that part of the township, the "West Eight Mile Community" was isolated from the rest of the township when Oak Park became a city.

The cost of segregation from the Oak Park district was funded by the federal government. The idea of busing children from the West Eight Mile Community to midtown Detroit was not sought by the families affected. Oak Park could not accommodate the new students into their existing building and either did not want federal money to build a high school that would have a relatively large black student population, or the cost to transport the students to Detroit was more cost effective. There is no documentation to confirm either scenario.

Smith went on to say that at the time the busing program began Northern High School was the closest Detroit school. Closer were Ferndale's Lincoln High School and Royal Oak's high school, later renamed Dondero High School after the districts' U.S. representative. At that time Representative Dondero's district included parts of Detroit's Eight Mile area. There were blacks attending Lincoln from the eastern section of the West Eight Mile

Community and an area along Hilton Road and Woodward Heights. The racial tensions during the time frame in which busing began created a comfort quota on the number of black students attending Lincoln. Attendance in Royal Oak was not a consideration.

About 1960 or 1961, parents had to get a court order to allow their children to attend Oak Park High School when the funding stopped. Talk about a tangled web of social engineering. Besides the housing situation, there was an enormous gap in educational opportunities for children living west of Wyoming. Separating east from west also created a political gap that would keep the community divided.

Around 1960, a brand-new model home was built in the township, which allowed the community to view what was coming and to place their preorders for new single-family homes yet to be built. The new housing boom started in earnest for the black community. The war houses came down, and new, beautiful, single-family homes went up. Those who could not afford to buy into this urban renewal had to move out.

Nevertheless, no amount of progress could erase the damage done to the psyche of a people held hostage by government policies that created the wall and the unwanted community.

Our Lady of Victory Mission

Our Lady of Victory Mission Church was constructed in the midst of this segregated housing development. It officially began with the appointment of Father Alvin Deem to head the black congregation. His Franciscan Order appointed him to assist the archdiocese in establishing a place of Catholic worship for blacks in the northwest area of Detroit. The archdiocese, under the administration of the Confraternity of Christian Doctrine, funded the mission.

Prior commitments delayed the arrival of Fr. Alvin until August 12, 1943. But when he came, he brought youthful energy, excitement, and a deep faith. When he volunteered to minister to the blacks, the young priest expected an assignment to a mission in Arkansas. Instead, Franciscan officials assigned him to the new mission for blacks in Detroit.

The control of the mission by the archdiocese was a problem from its inception. Our Lady of Victory was the only black mission that had to report to Monsignor Ryan and the Confraternity of Christian Doctrine. This scenario, Fr. Alvin believed, limited the effectiveness of the mission. Under the control of the Franciscans, the establishment of a mission school and the building of a permanent church would have been expedited. Fr. Alvin was moving fast with his ambitious plans for building a church and school, and the chancery appeared to be resistant to such a rapid expansion. Fr. Alvin told Smith in an interview that he felt the archdiocese was reluctant to encourage the development of the mission church.

In the meantime, he held Sunday Masses each week at nine-thirty in the morning while adult religious classes met on Wednesday evenings at seven-thirty, and religious instruction for children was held every Saturday morning at ten during the summer months at the Birdhurst Recreation Center.

In 1944, the mission had its first class receive the sacrament of Holy Communion; the celebrants included Sarah Jane McKenzie, Joseph A. Smith, and Betty White-Palmer. By the end of 1946, the mission moved into permanent quarters. The new church could seat over two hundred; however, according to Smith, the removal of Fr. Alvin would reduce the number of parish families to thirty-six.

The congregation, with the help of the Archdiocesan Development Fund, moved the old St. Juliana's Church to the donated land on West Eight Mile Road. By the time the parish was complete, there was a church, the rectory, the convent, the school, and acquisition of the Activity Hall building next to the church in October 1963.

The new Detroit mission served the black residents of the northwestern area of Detroit and Royal Oak Township. It was the fifth black parish in the history of the archdiocese. With the assistance of priests from Duns Scotus College, Fr. Alvin cleaned the 17-X-40-foot structure. Jerry McCarthy, a local Chevrolet dealer, supplied paint and painters. Donations for the mission came from various parishes in the city and suburbs. The first pews came from Gesu parish, and the communion rail from the Jesuits at the University of Detroit. Fr. Francis Stack of St. Mary Magdalene Church of Hazel Park donated a pump organ. It was positioned in a recessed wall at the back left side of the church.

The preparation of the church building required that Fr. Alvin solicit aid from all the parishes that had denied the black residents of the area the opportunity to worship in their churches. The Sisters of the Immaculate Heart of Mary again provided religious training. They sent the mission and summer school program five nuns to teach at Birdhurst Community Center.

During the summer of 1945, an unheard maximum of 450 children appeared for summer school, and two more nuns had to be called from Monroe, Michigan, to handle the crowd. Clearly, there was a critical need for a school and a church right away.

The solemn dedication of the new church took place on December 15, 1946, with Cardinal Mooney officiating and Msgr. John C. Ryan preaching the homily. This was a major historical event with bishops, priests, deacons, nuns, and other religious and civic leaders in attendance.

By 1947, there was a total attendance of about 226 parishioners at its peak. This number was good for a church in a constant state of turmoil. It is not surprising that the break in leadership stopped the parish's momentum, in spite of the fact that in one year with the Oblate sisters' presence, there were over one hundred baptisms.

Fr. Roberge goes on at length about how His Eminence invited the Oblate Sisters of Providence of Baltimore to come to Detroit. After quite a few letters back and forth, phone calls, and visits, Mother Theresa—the superior general—graciously accepted the invitation, and on Labor Day 1948, history was made when four Oblate nuns arrived in Detroit. An old house was acquired and remodeled to serve as a temporary convent. While modest, it was comfortable and featured a little devotional chapel, with walls decorated with murals by Allan Roben Crite, an accomplished black artist out of Boston, Massachusetts.

The coming of the Oblate Sisters marked the real progress in the work of conversion. The baptismal registry documents their evangelization efforts.

Baptismal Registry

1947 = 40

1948 = 23

1949 = 65

1950 = 106

1951 = 83

1952 = 64 to date

†

By the year 1951, the building of a Catholic community was in progress. A house and lot were acquired at 20468 Ilene to serve as a home for the janitor until the site was needed for the future school. By this time, increased attendance necessitated a third morning Mass at eleven on Sundays. By the 1950s, there were four Masses on Sundays: six-thirty, eight, nine-thirty, and eleven, and one on Saturdays at four in the afternoon. This shows how fast the church was growing.

There were approximately 450 people attending Mass on Sunday. There were 230 Catholic adults (sixteen and over) and 340 children in the parish. In addition, there were twenty altar boys actively serving at the Masses. The parish did not have its own cemetery.[2] Parishioners were buried at nearby Holy Sepulcher Cemetery in Southfield. Most churches have cemeteries or are affiliated with a church that runs one. OLV was affiliated with Holy Sepulcher and used its grounds for burial of the dead.

The erecting of a belfry and installing a set of electronic bells completed the church building, and it was an added attraction to the community. The bells rang for the first time on December 8, 1952. Those chimes could be heard all the way north in Royal Oak Township as far back as a quarter mile past Northend Street, which is where the projects extended. It was a beautiful sound so early in the morning.

In 1951, Our Lady of Victory had reached the status of an organized parochial unit with sufficient income to support itself.

> Our Lady of Victory was no longer the missionary parish it was when the confraternity first began to help it. The efforts of the resident pastor and the community of sisters have made it self-supporting.

This statement came in a letter from the chancellor to Fr. Hubert Roberge, telling him that Cardinal Mooney requested that he be notified of the new status of the church and that Msgr. Ryan was to be notified as well. With the change in status came the responsibility of paying the monthly salaries of at least two sisters and Fr. Roberge, as well.

Once the "mission" label was removed, the next step in the progression should have been the installation of Fr. Roberge as a permanent pastor of Our Lady of Victory parish. There is nothing to indicate that the parishioners ever knew this designation was made, and if they did they did not realize the significance of it, nor did they know that they could now at least make a request for a permanent pastor to be assigned to the parish.

✝

In order to build a Catholic community you must have stable Catholic leaders in the community who will lead by example. A vocation to religious life is one way to provide stable leaders who can teach and shape the community. If you fail in this regard, Catholicism and Christian living will not flourish.

The archives recorded its first vocations in September 1951. Charles Russell entered St. Maur Benedictine Priory as a lay brother candidate. There is no further information about what became of him. In 1952 Donald Cunningham, son of Mr. and Mrs. Thomas Cunningham, had also joined Russell, but he left and eventually married. The first student from the parish to enroll at Sacred Heart Seminary in 1952 was James Oldham. There is no record of what happened to him.

It seems that vocations were promoted through the Detroit Archdiocesan Council of Parish Sodality Unions. For example, on September 24, 1961, Our Lady of Victory saluted those sodalists who were continuing their Sodality affiliations in larger fields. They were Postulant Willa Dean Sumpter, who was pursuing a more complete Sodality life in the consecration of her life to Jesus through Mary as an Oblate Sister of Providence. Eleanor McConnel and Gwendolyn Jones transferred to Diocesan Adult Sodality. Benny Leonard (son of Washington Leonard) joined the U.S. Air Force, demonstrating his faithful allegiance to Sodality obligations. Beverly Glover transferred to Student Nurses Sodality at Providence Hospital in Detroit. Joining the Sodality prepared you for vocations in all occupations.

There were announcements made at Mass about religious vocations and booklets distributed to the congregation, but it did not take root at Our Lady of Victory. You had young men who thought about becoming priests but had no one to help them get there.

Jerry Rankin explains that being an altar boy exposed him and others to the idea of the priesthood as a vocation.

> Many of the boys felt that becoming a priest was more of a natural career goal in fulfilling a Catholic male role. We were taught to pray to find out if we had a vocation. There is not an easy explanation, but God calls people to his ministry as he chooses. Never in my wildest dream did I ever think that I would become a Baptist preacher! God knew otherwise.[3]

Foster Wilson Jr. recalls that a total of thirteen boys from other parishes in Detroit, including Our Lady of Victory, went to the seminary during a two-year period in the 1960s in hopes of becoming priests. All of them left! They never completed their training.

Garland Jaggers, author of *Fog: An Analysis of Catholic Dogma*, supports Foster's account but adds that all the boys were rejected. Having been the director of the Office of Black Catholic Affairs, he was in a position to know, because all the names had to pass through his office. So why did this happen? In his book, Garland touches on the many contradictions that are the Catholic Church.

Grace at Every Turn by Tom Honoré, certainly gives one another perspective of why there are so few black priests in the Catholic church in America today. Honoré's book is about being mulatto and Catholic in Baton Rouge, Louisiana, and his decision to join the Josephite Order. He recounts his reasons for leaving the religious order. Yes, there is racism even among the missionaries.

After reading Honoré's book, one may conclude that perhaps the missionary fathers wanted to save their souls, and not necessarily the black folks in their care. The mission is not to teach blacks how to look after themselves or make a living becoming pastoral leaders but to always remain in a perpetual state of need and dependence upon others. The black youngsters in their charge, according to Honoré were never invited to join the priesthood. He saw this as a contradiction to the missionary way of life everyone was aspiring to emulate.

Without going into details, the Josephite archives do document that the Archdiocese of Detroit produced two priests for the Detroit black community—Frs. Donald Clark and Tyrone Robinson; and the Holy Ghost Fathers produced one. But the momentum seems to stop there.

Fr. Alvin's mission was to make leaders for Our Lady of Victory's community and the world, and that he did. He allowed the members to grow to their full potential. For his reward, the archdiocese asked him to leave before his work was completed; yet they presented him with an award for his efforts. This appears to be a contradiction as well.

Why are there no black priests in any significant number? Perhaps all these contradictions leave us with more questions than answers.

Another way to build Catholic communities is to encourage involvement in the neighborhood. It appears that the Rev. Walter Bracken, who ministered to the small community from 1962 to 1965, made a sincere effort to foster the Holy Name Society and to encourage the men to be active in community affairs. On March 10, 1963, he called on the men to attend a very important meeting of the Mayor's Committee for Neighborhood Conservation and Home Improvement at the Detroit Housing Commission Office at West Eight Mile Road in Detroit. He wanted the organization well represented. Many new homes were going up over several years in the area surrounding the church. These meetings had a lot to do with the health of the neighborhood.

Those homes are still there, and they are still well maintained, but there is not a large number of Catholics living in the area any more.

The Committeemen of OLV were appointed by the Cardinal. Back in those early times, there was no parish council. The committee members acted as advisers to the pastor. They signed financial statements and served at the direction of the pastor. They were also members of the St. Vincent De Paul Society. The committeemen were known as parish council members after Vatican II, which was the start of change in the Catholic Church.

The only indication that there was a parish council was when Our Lady of Victory closed its doors, and an article in the *Michigan Catholic* in 1982 stated that a nine-member council approved the closing. Was the council composed of a mix of the two merged parishes? Let's hope that it was at least a fair ratio—not that it would have made a difference in the outcome.

†

In the matter of housekeeping, no records of any housekeepers were ever found. The small rectory had its history of housekeepers and maintenance staff taken from interviews and memories of the pioneers. A church building cannot function without them. The Carter interview revealed that the first maintenance staff was the Tommie Carter family, during Father Alvin's assignment. And, of course, Dolly White recalled that the James and Margaret Evans family was there during Fr. Roberge's assignment. James doubled as maintenance man and choir director.

Father Roberge's sister, who came with him, lived in the rectory to keep house and cook. She stayed on for DeCneudt's arrival and departed some time after that. Earline Wilson was Father's next housekeeper. She, along with her husband, Foster Sr., worked side by side in the church.

Then Sarah Dargin-Ware arrived and worked for about two years. Her son Norman Dargin went to the school and became an altar boy. Sarah said that DeCneudt was instrumental in getting her into nursing school. Because racism was so prevalent, she would not have had a chance on her own. She graduated in 1958 from Detroit Practical Nursing School. She lived in Royal Oak Township, east of Wyoming. Her family owned a home in Highland Park and had to leave because of the building of the Davison Freeway. In order to save their home, her father, who was a carpenter by trade, had it moved from Highland Park to Royal Oak Township. He acquired three homes in the township through bids. Sarah is now a member of St. Cecilia Church in Detroit.[4]

The last housekeeper for the rectory was Mary Elizabeth Robinson. She is a longtime member of the church and remains active. She served for Msgr. DeCneudt and departed some time during Fr. Bracken's assignment,[5] some time around 1962. She is currently active at the merged Presentation—Our Lady of Victory Church. She is a member of the choir and the Fifty and Over Club.

Bud and Darlie Bouie are another couple that had significant ties to the church. Darlie said, "We came to the church in 1948. Fr. Roberge was the pastor at the time. It was more like a family, because the church was so small."

Bud handled the repairs and maintenance of the church and school while Darlie helped out in the rectory from time to time. She was a cook and caterer for the church. She had the help of the women in the parish to assist her. Husband and wife were a team and very involved in parish life. Their two boys, Girard and Dennis, attended the school. Girard went into the seminary but decided it wasn't for him. The family moved out of the parish sometime in the 1960s. Darlie is presently at St. Girard in Detroit. Bud passed away in recent years.

True Measure of a Church

In order to understand what Our Lady of Victory is all about, one must become acquainted with the many parish activities and fund-raisers that went on. This reveals the pulse of a church that is moving forward towards sustainability and growth.

The parish finances were looking good for the times in 1951. The total operating income amounted to $16,582.85. Of this amount, $6,400.85 came from outside the parish. The rest was raised or contributed by the parishioners. By comparison, in 1949 they raised $7,561.00. For the year, on December 31, 1955, the receipts totaled $25,955.53, and expenses were 24, 303.41 with cash on hand and in bank of $1,754.04. Special collections were always taken up for the Indian and Negro Home Missions, and some of that money came back to the church.

There were fund-raising activities going on all the time. The Senior Sodality members sponsored the Pancake Breakfasts. Moreover, the Feather Party, always held in the church basement in the month of November, was an annual event that brought parishioners together during the Thanksgiving holiday season. Bingo, auctions, and prizes were the highlights. First prize was a big basket full of food and a large turkey. The Feather Party raised a lot of money. The men of the parish sponsored it, the women prepared the refreshments, and the sodality girls helped to distribute the food. The Holy Name Men were responsible for ticket returns. Every organization had its responsibilities.

There was the Parish Annual Homecoming Festival, again run by the men of the parish. This was held in the summertime. Committees were formed to handle the chores. They cooked up huge plates of ribs, and the women operated the booths and donated refreshments. Tickets were sold and top prizes of cars were given away, then gradually, money. The committee went after donations from area businesses, which were eager to give. Cole's Funeral Home always underwrote the printing of the tickets (See Appendix).

The 10th Annual Benefit Fund-raiser was held for the parish in May of 1957, given by Rosemary Gleason, a regular benefactor of the church. Rosemary represented the best in the region who wanted Our Lady of Victory to succeed.

There were the popular fish fries held once a week. Fish dinners were sold out of the church basement kitchen. Church law stipulated at the time that meat was forbidden on Friday, so those dinners were snapped up fast.

On December 6, 1959, a Waistline Apron Party was given for the benefit of the Oblate Sisters of Providence Motherhouse Building fund, sponsored by the Oblate Sisters of Providence Guild. Mildred Saunders was president at that time. Admission was determined by the size of your waistline. If your waist measured twenty-five inches, then you paid twenty-five cents. There were games, refreshments, and wonderful prizes. Gifts were available for purchase.

✝

What is a church without its worship services? There were the October Rosary devotions in the evening once a week with Arts and Crafts held for the children at the school. It was always getting dark early around October, so the children would get together in groups in the township and walk to church for rosary devotions. Back then, most folks didn't have cars.

There was the traditional Midnight Mass on Christmas Eve. Those Masses were packed to capacity, and most of the children were falling asleep, because it was so late at night. The Stations of the Cross were observed during Lent. It is a time to fast and pray for the coming of Jesus on Easter Sunday.

The Annual Parish May Crowning ceremony was always on the parish grounds. Adults joined the children in a rosary procession around the block. Services closed with an outdoor benediction of the blessed sacrament after the solemn Sodality crowning ceremony.

The St. Rita's Study Club met on Wednesday nights at seven-thirty. The discussion leader for the study club was Lillie Leonard. The general topic was The Coming of the Savior. Subtopics: The Annunciation of the Baptist. These discussion groups went on for weeks. In addition, there was a Story

Hour on Saturday afternoons. There were choir rehearsals and altar boy practices going on every week.

On January 15, 1959, Fr. Raymond J. Maiberger became the new administrator. He stayed only three years.

On Sunday, June 12, 1960, the eighth-grade graduation ceremony was held
at three in the afternoon. The graduates received communion in a group at the
nine-thirty Mass. The Rosary Altar Society ladies gave a lovely reception and
social after the ceremony. Fr. Hubert Roberge attended and took a photo with
the graduates on the church grounds. The first graduation to take place was a
historic moment.

In 1961, Cardinal Dearden appointed Fr. Walter D. Bracken administrator
of Our Lady of Victory. Fr. Maiberger transferred to St. Boniface in Detroit.
The parish rolls started to drop a little more even though there were still a
record number of baptisms documented—fourteen people at one time; and
twenty-two little ones made their first Holy Communion. School enrollment
was 242 pupils.

✝

The true measure of a church is determined not only by its sacramental
component, but also by its active organizations. Our Lady of Victory managed
to have up to twenty-one organizations up and running. They are listed in the
Appendix in the back of the book.

The Altar Boys' Society had no less than eight altar boys rotating two at a
time at each of four Sunday Masses; two altar boys served during the weekdays, and two served during devotions and special services, all on a rotating
basis. There were enough altar boys to fill the requirements of the parish.
They belong to the Altar Boy's Society.

Rankin recalls that Sr. Mary DePaul Yancey trained most of the altar boys
for years after the school opened its doors. Rankin became an altar boy in the
second grade along with Jerry Young (Sr. Sharon Young's younger brother).
Most of the boys were eager to serve. There were wooden tablets on the altar
with all of the responses printed on them in Latin; however, the boys had to
memorize every congregational response on that tablet before they could serve
Mass, and they all did.

The Boy Scouts went on a camping trip in 1949, accompanied by Scoutmaster James Gibson. The following article appeared in *St. Augustine's Messenger*:

> All Aboard! That was the call during the past summer in Detroit, Michigan, as the Greyhound "Special" drove up before the door of Our Lady of Victory Church. The scouts were going out. The photographer caught them as they lined up and filed into the bus. Present were Boy Scouts from a troop recently organized by Father McNeil at Holy Family Church, Inkster, Michigan, and scouts from troop 490 of Our Lady of Victory Parish. Their goal was Camp Howell, Brighton, Michigan, where they were to spend a happy two weeks camping in approved scout style. They were accompanied by Scoutmaster James Gibson, an active parish worker and a Knight of St. Peter Claver.
>
> The Boy Scout organization is one of the many activities sponsored by Holy Mother the Church in her continuous efforts to educate and train the minds and hearts of the young, to bring them close to God, and thus prepare them for the more serious activities of adult life.[6]

In 1951, they had thirty-five scouts. Mr. Maurice Foster was the scoutmaster at that time. The Boy Scouts met every Friday night.

The Girl Scouts were also formed and met on Tuesday nights at seven-thirty. Except for a photo, there was no additional information on their activities.

The Sodality was an organization made up of young people (boys and girls) to help them grow into good, lifelong Christians and incorporate their faith into their everyday lives, and it was supposed to be an avenue for religious life. Some of the girls became nurses, a couple became nuns, and others chose marriage or other careers. The boys joined the armed forces, became husbands, and some should have become priests.

On April 8, 1951, an article appeared in the *Church Bulletin*:

> One hundred and one Sodalists attended the Deanery meeting at Our Lady of Victory church. All the visitors expressed surprise and pleasure with our beautiful church and equipment. They were impressed with the food, as well.

Our Lady of Victory made a tradition of honoring those sodalists who continued their sodality affiliations in lifetime careers. The Senior Sodality was flourishing. The Junior Sodality grew larger after the opening of the school.

The men of the parish were a part of the Holy Name Society and sponsored Father and Son Breakfasts annually. If you didn't have a father, you got a substitute, which could be an uncle, godparent, or surrogate. They kicked off the event by going to Mass and receiving communion together. It was so Christian and so wonderful to see. The Holy Name Society's purpose was to promote Christian values and family togetherness. The men were very much the leaders of the parish—they handled everything. The women were the backbone and very much involved in their own organizations. The Mother-Daughter Banquets were held once a year and were sponsored by the men of the parish as well.

The Holy Name Society and the Men's Club encouraged all men and boys to be active in the Holy Name because its purpose was to bond them spiritually by their monthly Holy Communion Sunday and by a positive effort to respect the name of God. There was a liturgy committee (for readers at the Mass), an ushers committee, and a sick call committee (for visits, cards, rosary and pallbearers).

In October 1964, The Holy Name Society of Men held their election of officers: Washington Leonard, president; Foster Wilson Sr., vice president; Alex Pierce, secretary; James Anderson, treasurer. Appointments were made for the following committees: Razz Flowers, reader; and Al Cook, ushers.

The Men's Club was an organization that was vital to the social and financial formation projects and committees in order to help the parish. The annual Summer Festival Committee, the ADF Committee, a spring or autumn dance committee, the barbecues and fish fries were important fund-raising projects for the Men's Club. In working together for the interest of the parish, strong and lasting bonds are formed. Fr. Bracken stated, "We are not afraid to work on any given project, because we are doing it for God and his parish".[7]

The Rosary Altar Society and Confraternity of Christian Mothers called to order a meeting on January 11, 1962, to elect officers. The committees consisted of altar and linen chairmen, kitchen, special dinners and refreshments, supported by the Sodality Girls, Spiritual Development to name a few (Appendix).

There was a rotation of women who helped iron the church linens on a weekly basis. Some time in the mid 1950s, Darlie Bouie was the person to notify to schedule your time to serve. On November 13, 1955, a notice ran in the *Church Bulletin*: "Each woman of the parish considers it a privilege and an obligation to iron the linens of the altar at least once a year and do the same for the kitchen operations."

The Ladies Altar Society served a full breakfast on the second Sunday of every month and they prepared rolls and coffee on Sunday.

There were the Altar Society Guild appointments. They were divided up into territories: The Ferndale Guild, the East of Wyoming Guild, and the West of Wyoming Guild. There were chairpersons and co-chairs for these areas (see Appendix).

The Parent Teacher Association (PTA) of Our Lady of Victory School held its meetings on Sundays to support the school. Elections were held each year. The newly elected officers for 1964 were Alex Pierce, president; Al Cook, vice president; Maimie Pierce and Dorothy Henry, secretaries; Doris Robinson, treasurer.

The CYO Teen Club was functioning and held its election of officers. They were the Spiritual, Social, Civic/Cultural, and Athletic Committees (see Appendix).

The Oblate Sisters of Providence Guild president in the late 1950s was Almeta Carruth. She was featured in the *Oblate News and Views*, July 1959 issue. Mary Elizabeth Robinson was elected president at some point in the 1960s. She presented a Benefit Tea on May 5, 1963, at the Great Lakes Building to raise funds for the motherhouse in Baltimore.

In 1952, there was a sign of growth so strong at OLV that the garage house on the convent property was remodeled into an attractive clubroom to accommodate the various activities going on in the parish. Several hundred dollars was spent to furnish new space to hold more meetings.

Legion of Mary founder Callista Madeline Fortier was one of the early pioneers in 1946. Annette Zeppele worked with her on this committee. Madeline's son, Phillip, talks about his parents' role in Our Lady of Victory's beginnings:

> My father's full name was Charles Matthew Fortier, and people called him "Chuck" (1916–1975). He did not form the Legion of Mary, but my mother did. She went by her middle name, Madeline. My father used to help Fr. Roberge early on. Then he joined the Maryknolls but decided that wasn't for him, so he came back to Our Lady of Victory to offer his services. Fr. Roberge suggested he get active in the Legion of Mary, which was interracial. That was the unusual thing—to have an interracial Legion of Mary. It was there that he met my mother.[8]

Philip Fortier, M.M.A. is an adjunct professor, Department of Philosophy at University of Detroit Mercy.

The Carmelite Third Order consisted of priests, nuns, and lay people. On February 4, 1951, Our Lady of Victory Chapter of the Carmelite Third Order enrolled forty-three members. All members of the parish over sixteen years of age who desired to grow in the spiritual life were invited to join. Chapter conference was held once a month on the fourth Sunday in church. These notices were always printed in the church bulletin.

The church bulletin is the communication medium of a parish. It gives the members knowledge, understanding, and instructions of what is going on, and it is a permanent historical record of events as they occur. It was simply named *Our Lady of Victory Church Bulletin*. Much of the church's history can be found there. The custodians of history did the best they could to keep the bulletins in a safe place. Records between January 1951 and 1965 are held together by a large black spiral clasp, and therefore they are not well preserved. Some are in danger of disintegration. These records were never bound for permanent storage and preservation as in other parishes. Church bulletin records before January 7, 1951 and after 1967 could not be located, if there ever were any.

The January 1952 bulletin shows an insignia of the coat of arms of Pope Pius XII on the cover. The issue is printed on a mimeograph machine, and subsequent issues have similar religious pictures up until the issue of November 6, 1955. The cover of that issue shows a picture of the church building. A full page of advertisements started to appear at this time on the back cover.

Most of the businesses that advertised in the bulletin were around the West Eight Mile Community: James H. Cole Home for Funerals, Mark Cleaners & Dyers, The Jewel Box, Kat's Soda Bar, Richardson TV Sales & Service, Goldberg's Super Market, Lucky Boy Super Market, Veteran's Poultry (sold live and dressed poultry), and Thomas L. Hall Funeral Home, among others.

The mimeograph machine was no longer used, which allowed for more print and a cleaner look. This occurred during Rev. DeCneudt's assignment and continued until September 3, 1961, when it changed back to its old format. The ads were reduced in size and started appearing on the inside of the front cover. These changes took place during Fr. Raymond Maiberger's tenure. The nuns ran the mimeograph machine to print the bulletin, and the operation apparently moved from the rectory to the school office after it was built. There never was a secretary to do this work—just the nuns.

One cannot not help noticing the tone of the articles that appeared in the bulletin. It seems that the parishioners were regularly reminded to keep up their tithing and pay school tuition in a timely manner or were admonished if the collection went down. Maybe it was just the times.

Our Lady of Victory Federal Credit Union

Our Lady of Victory Federal Credit Union was located in the church basement. There was no documentation found of its beginnings, but a search turned up some old church bulletin articles in 1951 of the pastor announcing meetings to elect new officers to the board of directors. Why was it conceived? History has shown that the black community had such a hard time getting basic services that there was a great need to provide a lending institution that would serve their needs back in those turbulent days. Remember, the government was not giving out mortgages to black residents in the area. So it was an idea way ahead of its time and an innovative way to sidestep the status quo.

Our Lady of Victory's credit union appears to have been quite active for a while with new officers scheduled for election at the annual January meeting announced in the New Year 1951. It was emphasized that the success of the credit union depended upon active participation of its members. It had 118 members at that time. At this meeting, a report was made of the year's business. Members voted on what to do with the profit from the year's operation and elected new officers. The board of directors was comprised of six members (see Appendix).

Every year, a call went out to invite parishioners to acquaint themselves with the wonderful lending and borrowing agency flourishing in the parish. Members could invest their savings with interest far above the bank interest, and they were able to borrow with far less interest than you would pay at the bank. Savings were automatically insured for as much as the amount in the account without any extra cost to the depositor. Parishioners were always encouraged to stop downstairs after Mass and see Hattie Braddock so that she could explain procedures to them.

March 1952 the parish credit union had over $5,000.00 in assets and after paying all expenses showed a profit of $93.25. This was sufficient to pay dividends of 3½ percent. When the parish doors closed in 1982, the credit union died with it.

The Knights of St. Peter Claver—Santa Maria Council #105

The Knights of St. Peter Claver—Santa Maria Council #105 of Our Lady of Victory Church was organized some time around 1948, according to documents in the diocesan archives. The men were addressed as "brothers," and the women were addressed as "ladies."

The KPC, from its inception, was to be a black counterpart to the Knights of Columbus, and they were to provide black men with fraternal support and insurance benefits since southern blacks were denied membership in the Knights of Columbus.

There were fifty Knights and seventeen members of the Ladies Auxiliary recorded, but there was no installation date given. According to the records of Lady Marjorie Greene, Santa Maria Council #105 was established on February 6, 1949. That would appear to be about right since an organization had to exist to sponsor the Founders Day Forum scheduled for February 20, 1949. Lady Ruth Green-Leonard stated that she was the first grand lady of the Ladies Auxiliary some time between 1947 and 1949. She couldn't remember the exact year.

Keith wrote to His Eminence Edward Cardinal Mooney on December 6, 1947, requesting that he start the council in Detroit on behalf of the national office. He made a request to have the new order named after Cardinal Mooney, but it was declined, and the name became Santa Maria Council #105. The request is written on KPC letterhead, and Keith's official title is organizer for the northern district.

He was instructed by the national office to start the new chapter at Our Lady of Victory. Father Hubert Roberge had given his blessings and had pledged to be the chaplain of the Knights. Keith enrolled Catholic men from the ages of eighteen—thirty-five. The council was comprised of men from all the black parishes in the diocese. One of the strict rules required for membership was the observance of the sixth commandment of the church. The letter of request made note of the fact that the men in the parish were upstanding Catholics and good citizens and were quite capable of undertaking this responsibility.

Keith was convinced that these organized groups of young men were capable of promoting the phase of Catholic action that reflects favorable credit to both race and the church of Detroit. He unwittingly became the catalyst for the evangelization of black Catholics in the Detroit archdiocese on a much larger scale.

A Founders Day forum was arranged by Keith at the request of several outstanding civic leaders. It was held at the YMCA Branch at St. Antoine, and with the consent of Father Hubert Roberge, it came under the auspices of the Santa Maria Council 105.

February 20, 1949, was proclaimed Founders Day, celebrating the fortieth anniversary of the founding of the Knights of Peter Claver in 1909 by four Reverend Josephite Fathers; one of them being a Negro priest, the late Rev. John H. Dorsey, S.S.J., and six Negro Catholic laymen of the city of Mobile, Alabama. The first supreme knight was the late Gilbert Faustina, whose son was ordained to the priesthood in February 1947 and was a member of the Society of St. Edmund. He was assigned to teaching at St. Michaels's College at Winooski Park, Vermont.

A letter by Keith to Cardinal Mooney, found in the archdiocesan archives, describes the celebration in more detail. It was written on January 20, 1949:

> The theme of the celebration is the Negro's Contributions and Achievements in Catholicism. This observance will be emphasized by all Claverite members. It is the request of the supreme knight and the members of the Supreme Council that we celebrate this Founders' Day with high solemnity of the church, if possible. The celebration is to consist of Mass and the reception of Holy Communion in a body.
>
> The Founders Day celebration will be held at St. Joseph's Church, at Orleans and Jay Streets in Detroit, Michigan. The selection is to assist the pastor, Father Arnold F. Schneider, in promoting the colored apostolate in

that vicinity. There is a large class of candidates who are ready to embrace the faith.

Santa Maria Council #105 nurtured its spirituality by participating in church devotional services. On March 29, 1953, this notice was published in the bulletin:

> A custom that starts on Palm Sunday—Holy Thursday Adoration, requires members to maintain a vigil all day and all night. In keeping up the custom, the men of the parish, particularly the Knights of St. Peter Claver, are asked to sign up for the hours between midnight and five o'clock in the morning on a Friday. The women are asked to sign up for the day hours, particularly Friday morning.

The Knights did a fair amount of worshiping and praying, even pulling all night vigils as they practiced their faith in the name of St. Peter Claver. They were regularly featured on WJLB—FM radio on Tuesday evenings in the 1950s to recite the Rosary.

One of the charitable works that the Knights did was to purchase a station wagon for the Oblate nuns. They donated large funds to the church and school.

The council was a socially responsible organization. During the sixties they reactivated the Black Secretariat—a department within the Archdiocese of Detroit. It had been closed because the diocese didn't want to continue funding it. Today the department name has changed to the Office of Black Catholic Affairs.[9] It was created to address the needs of Black Catholics and provide a voice for them.

The members were participants in an organization called Metropolitan Organizing Strategy Enabling Strength (M.O.S.E.S.), which is dedicated to bringing mass transit to the region as well as addressing environmental and social issues of concern between city and suburban neighbors. There is strong participation in the St. Vincent de Paul Society to serve the needs of the poor. There is a presence in various ministries in the church with members bringing skills and expertise as they come to serve. They donate financially to the church.

The juniors collect toys for the needy and sick children. They serve at community soup kitchens and send donations to worthwhile causes.

The Ladies Auxiliary started to become more active in the 1950s. They had a membership drive and held their initiation ceremonies in OLV Church hall. Three women were initiated and received into the court on Sunday, March 16, 1952. They were Margaret Evans, Bessie Hodges, and Rosetta Bell. This may have been the revitalization of the Ladies Auxiliary.

In a conversation with the late Lady Jamesetta McCoy of Sacred Heart Court #71, it was revealed that OLV had the largest junior knights and daughters in the region. That was during the late 1980s and early 1990s. Branch Mother Denise Sears ran the Junior Knights Division, and the Junior Daughters were headed by Counselor Jackie Blakely, assisted by Betty Fulgiam. Unfortunately, the National office ended the Junior Knight Division here because their constitution allowed men only to organize it. In recent years, that ruling has been modified. The Knights and its junior division never fully recovered. Some of this can be blamed on the constant change in leadership and the lack of a strong layperson.

At some point, Santa Maria Council/Court #105 ceased to function. Foster and Helen Wilson reestablished it on February 19, 1977. OLV and Presentation had merged but had not physically combined the two churches. Foster could not explain why they did not take the original name except that it was an oversight, so the new Council became Our Lady of Victory—Presentation Council/Court #189. The area deputy was Willie Kelley for the council, and Annie Rosemond was deputy for the court. The pastor was Reverend Richard Hartmann (see Appendix).

In recent years, by consensus, the name was switched around to become Presentation—Our Lady of Victory Court #189. You can see the confusion that was created by the merger and leadership changes over the years. Perhaps if we had known our history, we would not have agreed so quickly to yet another change in name.

Finally, in the national communities, four black men were ordained as priests, and they were all members of the Knights of St. Peter Claver Organization. They were featured in the summer 2004 issue of *The Claverite*, a magazine published by the National.

The Knights of St. Peter Claver and its Ladies Auxiliary boasts a membership of 45,000 nationwide. The organization is the foundation of black Catholic life, with emphasis on strengthening the black community. It has been serving the needs of African American Catholics as well as being a support to pastors and bishops. It offers scholarships, mentor programs, and various contributions to worthwhile charitable organizations. The national organization had its headquarters temporarily in Montgomery, Alabama, because of Hurricane Katrina, which devastated their office in New Orleans, Louisiana, in 2005. The national office has moved back to its present location at 1825 Orleans Avenue, New Orleans. There is still not enough being done for the residents, particularly in the ninth ward, in New Orleans, and the residents of the Gulf Coast region are still in dire straits with the threat of matching funds being waived in Congress. A plea has gone out to the members to send donations and to contact their local representatives.

Our Lady of Victory School

The school building fund allowed the parish to raise money to construct a school. On March 29, 1953, an appeal went out for parishioners to be sure to use the special Easter collection envelope for the "Building Fund" of the proposed school. This was the first appeal to the parish for this fund. The parishioners' response would demonstrate to the pastor and to the cardinal just how earnestly they desire a school and their interest in this big project.

On April 19, 1953, the new pastor, Reverend Ferdinand DeCneudt, was welcomed into the parish family. The church was still in its infancy, a school was under construction, and Rev. DeCneudt was the third administrator to lead the parish. These accomplishments show the resourcefulness and strength of its pioneers under such trying circumstances.

This article ran in the bulletin on September 5, 1953:

> Wednesday, the Feast of St. Peter Claver, 1953, marks the opening for Catholic schools. Those children attending Madonna will come to Mass at seven forty-five. Parents are asked to see to it that their children are in church for the beginning of Mass Wednesday and every day during the school year. It is required that they are here for Mass if you expect them to ride the bus. If the child is late we ask you to please send a note stating the reason why. If your child does not attend Mass here each morning he or she MUST attend Mass at Madonna. We are working this year in a very special way for: Punctuality, neatness, good order, and good behavior. We need your cooperation, parents! Wednesday, Thursday, and Friday will be half-days of school this week at Madonna. The children will ride the bus to school after Mass, but the bus will not bring them back. Beginning Monday, September 14, they will go on a full-day schedule, and the buses will take them to and bring them from school each day.

The school was in the construction stage at this time, so all the children were sent to Madonna and St. Paul until the structure was ready, and that was not to be for another full year.

Dolly said that Our Lady of Victory was the first Catholic school system to have a kindergarten, because all Catholic schools started at first grade only. She especially remembered the kindergarten room with hopscotch and games in the tiles on the floor. "It was really something, and Fr. Roberge was very proud of that and the fact that he was instrumental in bringing the colored nuns from Baltimore to staff the school."

When Father DeCneudt arrived, the school was completed and ready to open on September 13, 1954. There was a ground-breaking ceremony, and pictures were taken of the historic event. A ceremony for the laying of the cornerstone took place on June 20, 1954. Officiating was Fr. DeCneudt and assisting were Father Leo Smith, Charles Selens, a contractor, and Gerald Diehl the architect.

The school opened with kindergarten, first, and second grades. According to Jerry Rankin, the first few weeks of school was held in the basement of the church because the construction of the school was in the final stages. The grand open house was held on September 26, 1954. The children attended Mass and then marched in step like little soldiers to their classrooms by nine in the morning.

A noteworthy piece of information was the hiring of the first and only lay teacher in 1959. Her name was Naomi Ruth Anderson, and she taught fourth grade. She was a longtime member of the church and remains active to the present day.[10]

The children of Our Lady of Victory donned their new uniforms for the first time, and it was a wonderful sight to see. The girls wore dark blue jumpers with the OLV emblem on the left hand side of the chest, with white, short-sleeved cotton or polyester blouses. The boys wore dark blue pants, white shirts, and blue ties. All the fund-raisers, school building funds, and donations held for a number of years finally made this dream a reality.

Mr. and Mrs. Edward Wilson donated a beautiful flagpole that was placed in front of the building. During a dedication ceremony, the flag was hoisted for the first time in the fall of 1956. The school was up and operating, and added two grades a year. By 1960, it was taking children up to the eighth grade. The church revolved around the school and the school reflected the teachings of the church.

The entire student body collected S&H Green stamps for the sole purpose of purchasing a bus and anything else that the school needed. Collecting these stamps was a way to make purchases of quality products without spending a lot of money, which was a common practice in those days. After years of collection drives, the goal was reached. Can you imagine buying an expensive bus with stamps today?

Mother Stella Marie taught for only two years, and then Mother Mary Patricia replaced her. Students got a very good basic education, and the Oblate Sisters of Providence were the big reason. Parents took religious instructions as a prerequisite for getting their children in the school. About 95 percent of the school was Catholic. This community was becoming a Catholic Community.

There was the spare room, so called because it was an empty room—not used for classes but as a music room with a grand piano. Mother Stella Marie taught the students how to sing in Latin for the High Mass on Sundays. She taught square dancing, folk songs, and practiced hymns in that spare room, and she taught poetry. Students were taught how to speak and be courteous when guests came to the classrooms. They said the Pledge of Allegiance without fear of violating someone's civil rights. Students were not forced to go to the school; they came because they wanted to be there. Parents lined up trying to get their children into the new school.

Mass was offered five days a week, and all of them were full of children from all the grades. There was always a visiting priest to assist the pastor, because the rectory was too small to accommodate another live-in priest.

Time changes things, and Our Lady of Victory was beginning a transformation. A letter of concern was addressed to the parish that had to do with parents of other faiths sending their children to the school and not fulfilling their obligation to attend a series of adult instructions in the Catholic religion and Sunday Mass attendance. Five priests had been assigned to the church by this time, and on July 21, 1963 in the church bulletin, Fr. Bracken addressed his concerns:

> Children will be removed in the fall if parents do not comply. To teach these little ones Christianity in the classroom and then destroy their faith by the non-Christian conduct at home is a scandal! And woe to those who scandalize these little ones.

Different personalities bring different agendas. Some priest cared about the church, and some may have been indifferent. As a priest, if you know that you are only going to be in a church for a short time, you learn not to become involved. People can tell when they are cared about and when they are not. People leave when they feel that their needs are not being met. When that happens, children are removed as well.

Rules began to change. What worked before was not working now. It takes dynamic leadership to keep the flock connected to the faith, and, unfortunately, that leadership stopped being encouraged or nurtured among the membership. That notice may or may not have reached the non-Catholics who were not in compliance if they did not attend the church. If the policies that dealt with this issue had been enforced when these parents were enrolling their children, this neglect would never have had a chance to take root. Leadership has to be stable in order for that to happen.

This notice demonstrates that a shift was occurring in the seriousness of attending the school. Times were changing, and morals were changing, too. Even though Fr. Bracken tried hard to make good Catholics, he had the deck stacked against him. You can't perform miracles if you are only there for a short time … not in a black church … not in any church! The archdiocese's policy of assigning a priest of a different ethnicity to a black Catholic Church was just not always a good thing. They wouldn't stand for it in a white church. This is a point that no one has ever discussed.

With the threat of a school closing looming, parents lead the fight to keep it open. It worked for a little while, but eventually the school closed in June 1970.

There was evidence in the archives of a decline in enrollment of children at Our Lady of Victory School. The historical data of 1959 listed these reasons:

Low IQ
Academically deficient
Distance
Unable to afford tuition

Apparently the leadership, which determines policy, is not an important enough factor to consider for declining enrollment. Looking at these reasons, perhaps it should have been.

Old St. Juliana was donated to Our Lady of Victory and trucked to its new site on Washburn and West Eight Mile Road, where it was placed on the poured foundation.

Holding up Blessed Mother statue from L to R: Robert Thomas and Sam Smith. Visible in second row, James MaHaley. Third row altar boys Frank Cryer and James Benjamin. Visible in fourth row, William Rankin.

The mission church. An exterior view.

An interior view of the tastefully decorated church.

The exterior and interior view of the convent home for the Oblates.

1955. Our Lady of Victory Sodality Breakfast.

First Communion Class of 1953.

First Communion Class of 1960.

Sarah Dargin-Ware, housekeeper.
Photo supplied by Msgr. Ferdinand DeCneudt.

Tommie Carter, first maintenance staff.
Photo supplied by Ona Carter-Harris.

Legion of Mary barbecue. Far left Martha Palms-Williams. Hands folded Willie "Bud" Bouie. Center Father DeCneudt. Cutting ribs Foster Wilson Sr. with wife Earline standing behind him.

December 15, 1946. Solemn dedication of the new church. Altar boy, Edward Wilson Jr., Edward Cardinal Mooney, and Farther McMahon.

Halloween Party 1961. King Arthur Green and
Queen Lorna Wilson-Thomas.

December 2, 1950. Byron-Norwood Nuptials,
Fr. Hubert Roberge officiating.

Boy Scouts photo was featured in *St. Augustine's Messenger*,
December 1949 edition.

Girl Scouts. Jean Smith-DuPlessis is holding the flag.

April 16, 1950. The Knights on a trip to Toledo, Ohio.

L to R: Unidentified knight, Fr. DeCneudt, Judge Wade McCree, James Cole, and Luther Keith. These Knights were the movers and shakers in Detroit.

Santa Maria Council #105 at picnic Inkster, Michigan.

1981. KPC Ladies Auxiliary Our Lady of Victory—
Presentation Court #189.

October 31, 1953. Rosary Hour, Knights of
St. Peter Claver, WJLB Radio.

February 21, 1954. Ground-breaking for historic school.

1954 School dedication ceremony. Edward Cardinal Mooney officiates. Standing to his right are Fr. Roberge and Fr. DeCneudt.

June 20, 1954. Historic laying of the cornerstone for the new school.

1964 - OUR LADY OF VICTORY SCHOOL - 1965
Detroit, Michigan

Our Lady of Victory School. It was a wonderful asset to the community.

The school building as it appears today in a state of disrepair and a blight on the community.

Historic first graduating class of 1960.

1954. First graders on opening day of new school are taught
by Mother Providencia.

Fifth and sixth graders featuring future first graduates.

Sources

1. Fr. Hubert Roberge, ed. Financial Data, Our Lady of Victory Archives. 1952.

2. "Parish Census." Archdiocese of Detroit Archives. 1954.

3. Jerry Rankin, e-mail. 9 September 2005.

4. Sarah Ware, telephone interview. 18 April 2004.

5. Mary E. Robinson, telephone conversation. 2004.

6. "Two Weeks in the Woods," *St.Augustine's Messenger.* 28 (1949), 219.

7. "Fr. Bracken and the Men's Club," *Our Lady of Victory Church Bulletin*, 13 June 1965.

8. Philip Fortier, e-mail. 4 October 2004.

9. Foster Wilson Jr., home interview. 21 October 2004.

10. Naomi Anderson, home interview. 20 March 2004.

IV

The End of an Era

Introduction

In Part IV, the focus will be to understand what happened to Our Lady of Victory in comparison with the other black churches of the times. You will learn the story behind Presentation, which was an all-white parish that went through demographic changes. A disturbing pattern will emerge of black churches closing down on a regular basis. The fate of OLV was just one more example of the tragedy that has befallen the black Catholics in the Detroit area.

All of the black parishes that started out in the World War II era were labeled "mission" churches. Eventually, the archdiocese took these missions over, and they closed with the exception of Sacred Heart and a few other churches left standing after white migration out of the neighborhoods took place on a massive scale. The lack of black archdiocesan priests led to the closing of many of the black churches, because there was no one to staff them.

You will come to understand why it is important to know about St. George and St. Benedict the Moor and Holy Ghost because of their similarities to OLV.

Also in this section, it is revealed that St. Benedict the Moor was founded by Fr. Norman Dukette, who is a black priest, and that his was the second African American parish established specifically to serve the black community. The Holy Ghost fathers took over that parish and later the Josephites. Why was the only black priest in the diocese removed? Does it make sense? He had to start from scratch building a church and evangelizing in Flint. He did it and remained there for many years.

Comparing these parishes and getting an understanding of what happened to them will give you a better understanding of the difficulties Our Lady of Victory had to face, and while her issues are unique, she was never alone in this struggle.

Presentation Church

Fr. Thomas McMahon founded Presentation Parish in 1941. The first Mass was celebrated on July 13, 1941, at the University of Detroit High School. In October of that year, ground was broken for the current church. The first Mass was celebrated in the new church on April 16, 1942 and it was formally dedicated on June 7, 1942.

Within several years, Presentation's congregation had opened a school staffed by the Dominican Sisters of Adrian. The parish served a predominately white population, and Fr. McMahon was the pastor for fifteen years. The Rev. Stanley Shafer became the pastor in 1956 and was there for thirteen more years to 1969.[1] The story told is that Fr. Shafer was not happy about the merging of the two parishes and resisted it as long as he could. He was gone by the time the two parishes merged, and Msgr. Thomas Finnegan became the administrator over the two parishes.

The demographics of the area were starting to change, and it was becoming predominantly black with the white population shifting to the surrounding suburbs. With these changes, the vision of the archdiocese began to change, and the merged church began experiencing a turnover of administrators who were not allowed to stay any length of time, just as it had been at Our Lady of Victory. This in turn caused an exodus of people who were tired of the constant change. The parish suffered neglect and a financial debt that was eventually forgiven when a three-parish merger took place. It wasn't enough to stop the erosion of church membership. The cycle of leadership instability came to a halt with the appointment of the parish's first deacon.

Presentation School suffered even more with relaxed restrictions and the dismissal of the last Oblate Sisters' presence by yet another administrator, Randy Phillips. Tuition skyrocketed, and, to make matters worse, quality suffered. Parents started sending their children to schools that reflected their values. The merged church had no incentive to support the school, which began to resemble little of what the members had known.

Eventually the education committee had to make a decision to either close the school and sell the building or lease it. The building was leased, and that is the present status of the school.

Ironically, the deacon is an OLV alumni ... baptized as an infant. He is the Rev. Mr. Hubert Sanders, Administrator of Presentation—Our Lady of Victory Church. A priest contracts annually to say Mass on Sundays.

Courtesy of Presentation Archives

The Beginning of the End

The beginning of the end came to Our Lady of Victory. By 1970, the school was closed, and the students and the Oblate Sisters of Providence had settled in at Presentation School where Dominican Nuns were already on staff. Just imagine the tension that must have surfaced when that happened. You cannot force people to mix and expect that everything will be smooth, because it won't. If the Archdiocese of Detroit never permitted mixing among its own kind, why force a mix with the black church? The logical solution would be to help a struggling church increase its odds of surviving independently.

The "mission" label was removed once the church obtained parish status, but was there a plan to eventually close the church and school? Because that's just what happened! Our Lady of Victory was a community made up of working, two-parent households. There is no good reason why it should not have been a sustainable Catholic church except that maybe it was just a little too close in proximity to Presentation once that parish started changing. The whites were moving out of the area, and blacks were allowed to move into the community and the church.

From the archdiocese's perspective, in terms of economics, one of the churches had to go. Were the reasons for Our Lady of Victory's existence no longer valid? There was certainly an escalation of priest turnover at this point to prove it. They were staying sometimes for only two or three years.

With white flight out of the city of Detroit, the rules that governed Catholic schools had begun to relax. That commonality that used to be prevalent in the past, that made Catholic schools so special, was now lacking. At Our Lady of Victory there was one last effort to keep the school as Catholic as possible. This plea appeared on August 8, 1965:

Already people's thoughts are turning to school, and they are asking if they can enroll their children in our school in September. For the benefit of all who desire information on this subject, I will state the policy of Fr. Bracken and of other pastors before him, which I also intend to follow, and it is this: Only those who show an interest in the Catholic faith themselves and actively support the parish can be permitted to have children in our school. This policy is necessary for a number of reasons: 1) we do not receive any tax funds to run our school; it must be operated solely on tuition and the contributions of Catholics. It would therefore be unfair to allow anyone to impose on others by not doing his share. 2) It is not logical for parents who are not Catholic and who are not interested in the Catholic faith to place their children in a Catholic school where the Catholic religion is taught. We insist therefore, that they (or at least one parent) take a complete course of instructions in the Catholic faith, and attend Mass regularly and faithfully on Sundays.

After the merger in 1975, it seemed that anybody could attend Presentation school no matter what his or her faith was. Before 1970, there was a rumor that if you were an outsider, you were evaluated with a test, and of course you had to take instructions before you could get into Presentation school. They didn't make it easy. At Our Lady of Victory you had to take instructions.

By 1982, the merger was complete at Presentation—Our Lady of Victory church. As time passed, some parents started moving their children to other schools while still attending the home parish. It was not something that was spoken about. But you could see that the parishioners were not happy about the changing policies in the school. They did not seem to feel that they had a stake in the school anymore. They started putting their children in schools that they thought were more in sync with their faith and beliefs.

In the early years at Our Lady of Victory, the parishioners were fortunate to get four to five very good priests, but sadly as time marched on, they got some lemons as well. The church body grew around the school! All the catechism instructions, all the baptisms, all the faithful Mass attendance, all the fundraising was to get your children into Our Lady of Victory School. When the school closed, it killed the spirit of the church. It just took the wind out of everything the members were trying to accomplish; with leadership change escalating in frequency, the membership went through further erosion.

Leatrice Robinson, a Presentation parishioner at this time, became the new owner of OLV school from 1978 to 1993. It was called Robinson Advantage Institute. It became A Step Ahead, an offshoot from Robinson Advantage and was set up in the Activities Building. Leatrice was giving the employees an opportunity to go into business. They would work with the kindergarten class only.

Then in 1993, she retired, and A Step Ahead took over until around 2001 or 2002. They moved out of the Activities Building to the present location on Livernois Avenue in Detroit. The vacant, boarded-up school building and the Activities Hall next door to the church are in the hands of yet another private owner. The church building was sold to another denomination, which is currently holding services there today.

All three buildings should be declared historic landmarks because of their unique African American Catholic heritage.

The Merger

The Archdiocese of Detroit had no incentive to keep Our Lady of Victory open since there were no black priests to run it. As far back as the late 1950s, people were being steered to Presentation when they moved into the vicinity of both parishes, which were less than a mile apart. When Presentation opened up to blacks, the whites escalated their moves into the surrounding suburbs. Nowhere in the history of the church did you find any other ethnic group forced to attend another parish. They are either a cluster parish or a closed parish. Cluster parishes operate kind of like the merged Presentation—Our Lady of Victory of 1975. One priest serves two separate parishes, and services are adjusted accordingly.

What has happened in subsequent years to the merged church has caused personal distress to the members. At one time, Presentation—Our Lady of Victory had a large number of prominent and well-to-do black Catholics. So many people have left. Some went quietly, and one gentleman stood in front of church and announced that he was never coming back after one priest too many was assigned. The numbers have gone down substantially over the years.

Our Lady of Victory officially merged with Presentation in 1975, but the parishioners remained in their own buildings. Masses continued at Our Lady of Victory and at Presentation until the final closing holy hour on August 1, 1982. Madre Anna Bates was in attendance. There was a walking and motor procession of the blessed sacrament from Our Lady of Victory to Presentation at Pembroke and Meyers. Mother Bates was surely saddened by this turn of events. Mae Ruth Little said, "The members were crying so hard ... it was very sad. They did not want to go to Presentation. They wanted their church and school back." She was there when the church was in a storefront and witnessed the move to the new site. She and her husband (deceased) raised three boys and were an integral part of church life.

172

Some folks claim that Our Lady of Victory was debt-free at the time of the closing. There are others who say—not so! If there was a debt, it was caused by unstable leadership. And since I had no access to documentation to substantiate the claim, you are free to draw your own conclusions. Only those who were privy to the information know the real story.

Somehow, it really doesn't matter, because finances were never the real issue—support for the black church was and always will be the real issue!

✝

Anybody can see the havoc that was unleashed when demographics changed. It shows how the city of Detroit suffered financially and spiritually. An editorial written in the *Michigan Catholic* clearly shows how the Archdiocese of Detroit reluctantly tolerated its flock's contribution to white flight. It also carried large real-estate ads in the 1950s boasting beautiful, single-family homes in developing suburban Catholic communities as the selling points. Whites feared that their properties would go down with blacks moving into their neighborhoods. The following portion of an article that appeared sums it up:

> Some Catholic families reside in the city because of the former shortage of Catholic school facilities in suburbs and small towns. However, this situation is rapidly changing hereabouts as many suburban parishes are building schools and churches.[2]

White flight began in earnest with whole Catholic neighborhoods picking up and moving out. Now there is evidence of the archdiocese trying its best to stem this tide. In its Opinion Columns it chastised its members on the need for tolerance, "and to accept the Negro as part of the mystical body of Christ, if you are truly going to call yourselves Christians. Race prejudice is not only bad morals; it is an extravagant and uneconomical luxury that Americans cannot afford."[3] The archdiocese tried to assure the white Catholics that there was no need to sell simultaneously because that is what creates deflated housing values. While the general population knew that whites had left the city, no one thought or even connected that Catholics were the biggest part of the migration.

Now the chasm is even wider between city and suburbs, and development is growing for Catholic churches and schools in the outer rings of Detroit, leaving the inner city to struggle financially. There is a greater need than ever before for parochial schools, which are famous for their excellent education. The focus should be primarily on this objective.

What has taken place in Detroit is a complete relaxation of the rules that governed Catholic schools and made them unique. This finished off what was left of a dwindling Catholic community in Detroit. There are no conditions placed on parents who enroll their children in parochial schools—no studying of the faith, no prerequisites are required to attend as was required at Our Lady of Victory. Black Catholics no longer feel compelled to support their schools, because they bear little resemblance to what they had come to expect in a parochial school.

If the government had given mortgage loans to blacks to build their dream homes, and if the church had pursued this un-Christian behavior as zealously as it pursued abortion and gay marriages and Proposition A, it could have been a staunch crusader in shaping and building whole Catholic communities and Christian lives in the city of Detroit today. After all, that is the trademark of the Catholic Church.

Proposition A was a proposal placed on the ballot in order to get public funding for private schools, and it failed. Public funds would have helped the diocese overcome the deficits that plagued inner city schools. The diocese was supportive of this proposal and went all out appealing to its members to vote yes. They voted against it. In people's minds, it was in direct conflict with the separation of church and state doctrine that is cemented in the American way of life.

Just fast-forward to the year 2006 and see how many schools have already closed in the city of Detroit. Flight out of the city has gotten so bad that even the folks living in the suburbs are beginning to question urban sprawl and the environmental impact on the land and its resources. Yet the Archdiocese of Detroit still does not have a plan to address this growing problem.

Just take a page out of Our Lady of Victory's story. There is still an education crisis going on in Detroit, and parents are scrambling for good schools. Since the failure of Proposition A, Catholic schools are closing at an alarming rate just when the need is greatest.

The Other Black Churches

So far, we presented three other black churches that were set aside for blacks in the region during the forties. And it might have remained just something to be mentioned had it not been for a telephone conversation with Fr. Hogan from a referral by the Oblate Sisters of Providence Archives. He was recommended to expand the research on Our Lady of Victory. Fr. Hogan is a Josephite priest, and his order played an important role in the early days of the black church. His materials revealed the Josephite's history in the black community. They had a presence in Detroit from 1949 to 1973.

Three churches were already in existence at the time of Our Lady of Victory's beginnings. They were Sacred Heart near downtown east; Holy Ghost, northeast side; and St. Benedict the Moor on the west side. But there was also another church that had black membership. It was St. George Catholic Church at Westminster and Russell in Detroit.

"Judging from the slow pace at which the Archdiocesan Church began to address itself to the black community, one can assume that it was not a popular task. When the bishop did give his approval, he frequently turned to a religious order, rather than diocesan personnel. The tradition for this goes back to the Second Plenary Council of Baltimore, held in 1863. There the bishops of the United States issued a call to the Josephite Fathers of England to preach the gospel in the black community. In the mid-nineteenth century, diocesan clergy were still few in number in this country. Many young dioceses like Detroit had to rely on religious orders to staff parishes.

Bishop John Foley granted Fr. Joseph Wuest CSSp permission to open the St. Peter Claver Mission. Fr. Wuest was from a religious order used to staff the churches in the black community. Each time a new mission began, an order priest was assigned—Holy Ghost Fathers at St. Peter Claver, Holy Ghost, and Holy Family; and a Franciscan Friar at Our Lady of Victory. The only exception is St. Benedict the Moor, established by Fr. Norman Dukette—a black archdiocesan priest—at the direction of Bishop Michael Gallagher.

The Holy Ghost Fathers also gave the archdiocese its second black priest, Father Leonard Cunningham from South Carolina. Father served at Holy Ghost Church from 1955 to 1959 for five years as an associate pastor to Fr. Thomas Clynes."[4]

When Fr. Dukette was sent to Flint, the archdiocese replaced the only black archdiocesan priest in Detroit. There seem to be no vision to staff black churches with black personnel. It was too logical for Father Dukette to stay at St. Benedict the Moor which desperately needed a permanent pastor.

Sacred Heart

"The move from St. Peter Claver to Sacred Heart began with the transfer from the apartment, the rectory, and the school to Sacred Heart School. The Felician Sisters moved into the convent. They added one classroom each year until there was a complete grade school and high school staffed by twelve sisters. The sisters recalled a crowded building, but problems were comparatively small and few in number. The situation was made more agreeable because of the cooperation between teachers and parents. Parents from around the city sent their children to the one school where black children could be enrolled. Parochial schools were known for their good discipline and educational opportunities, and that was highly valued.

There was no religious requirement for admission, save an understanding that religion would be taught. Father Thiefels, and the Holy Ghost Fathers as a whole, looked on a school as a primary means for reaching converts in the community.

Financial support came from other parishes on the eastside of the city, and through the ingenuity of Fr. Thiefels and the sisters. Since the Felician Sisters were and are primarily a Polish order, a great deal of support came from the Polish parishes. The sisters themselves received no salary from the parish, but the motherhouse supported them. In those early days, the school charged no tuition.

It was not until some months after the Felician Sisters moved into the convent at Sacred Heart that they began to take on the task of religious instruction for children attending public schools. Until then, it had been handled by Mary Schutz, who had joined the Catholic Instruction League. It was during this time that Fr. Clynes began saying Mass in a home on the city's northeast side. It was not long before some of the sisters were accompanying him and having catechism classes while the adults were socializing after the Mass.

When the parish was officially established, and a school opened, the Felician Sisters staffed it with Sr. DePorres as the first principal. The classes were combined—first and second, third and fourth, fifth and sixth, etc. When the school was completed, between 300 and 400 pupils attended."[4]

Today Sacred Heart is a thriving parish. It has an innovative priest in Reverend Norman P. Thomas, who has been at the parish for practically a lifetime—over thirty years. It is rather interesting that he is listed as an administrator on the archdiocesan web site. The black parish boasts a membership numbering 1,327 families.

Holy Ghost

"The parishes, which grew up for black Catholics, have the appearance of a family with each generation giving birth to a new generation. The small group gathering in the classroom of St. Mary School with Fr. Joseph Wuest gave way to St. Peter Claver, and that to Sacred Heart. From St. Peter Claver, St. Benedict the Moor was grafted onto the west side of the city. As the city expanded, new missions grew on both sides of Woodward Avenue. One grew directly from St. Peter—Sacred Heart. Like its mother church, Holy Ghost Mission was pastored by the Holy Ghost Fathers.

The other (Our Lady of Victory) developed independently of any of the older communities. Still another appeared in the suburban community of Inkster rooted in the rich fertile faith of St. Benedict the Moor Mission.

A parishioner's home served as a gathering place for worship in the mid-thirties. Fr. Thomas Clynes, CSSp, came out of Sacred Heart to hold catechism classes in the area of Ryan Road and East Seven Mile, and gradually built a small community.

From a house, the small group moved to a storefront at Klinger and Stockton Streets. Here fifteen families worshiped for nearly a year until the basement of the new church building was completed. Edward Cardinal Mooney dedicated it in the spring of 1944. The entire building was never completed, and the congregation moved from the same basement church to the nearby parish hall. The old basement church became the social hall.

The mission grew with the addition of a school from 1945 to 1946. Five Felician sisters served the eight grades. With the attraction that the school

held for the community, the congregation grew until two priests were necessary to serve its needs, and they scheduled four Masses each Sunday.

The Holy Ghost Fathers served the parish until the archdiocese assigned
Bishop Thomas Gumbleton there as pastor in the late 1960s. The church did
not receive full parish status until that time."[5]

A parishioner of Presentation—Our Lady of Victory, Evelyn Purdue,
migrated from Holy Ghost Church. She said that after they finally built the
new church on the basement foundation, the church closed its doors not long
after that.

St. George Catholic Church

Besides Sacred Heart, Holy Ghost, and St. Benedict the Moor, there was one
more church on the near east side—St. George. It was formally a Lithuanian
church established in the early 1890s that later served the needs of an all-
Negro mission staffed by the Josephite Fathers.

"When the Sisters Home Visitors of Mary was established in 1949 by Sisters Mary Schutz and Agnes, they took up residence in St. George's convent
for the sole purpose of evangelizing the black community. This produced a
congregation of up to a thousand at its peak before it closed.

St. George Church, located at 1313 Westminster, was established for the
spiritual needs of the Lithuanian people on the east side of Detroit. It had a
long, flourishing life, but by the 1940s, most of the Lithuanian population had
moved to the west side.

In 1949, Cardinal Mooney assigned territorial lines to the parish and
invited the Josephite Fathers to assume responsibility. St. George, bordering
on a Detroit factory district was a mission church. The plant consisted of a
large church with a basement hall, and an eight-classroom school, which was
closed for four years. It had a rectory and a convent. The parish area contained
fifteen thousand people, mostly African-American, very few of whom were
Catholic. A Josephite priest, Father Henry Offer, S.S.J., a native of Detroit
from St. Agnes parish, was appointed pastor. The first Mass was on Christmas of 1949, with an attendance of seventy-five.

In 1949, the Sisters Home Visitors of Mary was established for the evangelization of African Americans. They visited families door-to-door throughout
the parish. They also taught Sunday school.

To meet the recreational needs of the area, Father Offer opened the church
basement to the children of the community and established a roller rink, box-

ing, and other activities, which became tremendously popular. By the end of the first year, the congregation increased to 525.

On Sunday, December 31, 1950, the boys and girls of St. George's Church hosted a Christmas party for approximately 250 scouts. Among those present were troop No.1 from Holy Family, Inkster; troop No. 490 from Our Lady of Victory, Detroit; and the newly organized Girl Scout troops from both parishes.

The guests were entertained with movies and by a magician, and with stunts and songs from the various troops. The party was under the able leadership of Mr. James Gibson, whose good work among the Boy Scouts was well-known in Detroit. Present at the party were Father Henry Offer of St. George and Father Hubert J. Roberge of Our Lady of Victory.

In September of 1950, two classrooms were refurbished, and St. George's school was reopened with two grades and 110 students. The Immaculate Heart of Mary Sisters staffed the school, and by 1955, it reached an enrollment of 243. In this same year, the Annual Report indicated a congregation of 993. During St. George's fifteen-year life as a Josephite parish, 906 were baptized.

St. George produced one black priest, Fr. Tyrone Robinson, and Sr. Elizabeth Harris of the Home Visitors of Mary. They were inspired by the ministry there. Fr. Robinson had an assignment at Presentation—Our Lady of Victory from 1985–1989.

In the 1960s, population shifts once again began to affect St. George's parish. Extensive redevelopment projects had diminished the population of the area. In 1965, a massive freeway development (the Chrysler Freeway) took over the property of the parish. The last Mass at St. George took place on August 29, 1965. The parish was dissolved and parishioners were reassigned to neighboring Santa Maria and Blessed Sacrament Cathedral Parishes.

Fr. Edward Walsh, who had been at the parish only two years, assailed the freeway policy in his final sermon. He charged, "There is never any consideration given to the moral nature of this institution in this community. Today we have a crying need for better schools and conditions, and what do they do? They tear down the school and church." [8]

He explained later that the parish had a membership of a thousand when the parishioners were reassigned to Santa Maria and Blessed Sacrament. The parish had been a Negro mission since 1950, a special apostolate of the Josephite Fathers. In 1964, knowing that St. George was closing, the Josephites, with Fr. Patrick Veale as pastor, took over the administration of St. Benedict the Moor Parish.

St. Benedict the Moor

"The growth of Detroit in the 1920s brought a diverse population. The foreign-born accounted for most of the city's population increase between 1920 and 1925, and this last great stream of immigration included Catholic groups that had not been represented in the diocese. Like his predecessors, Bishop Gallagher was generous in his provision for foreign-born parishes. Thirty-two of the ninety-eight parishes established in the diocese between 1918 and 1929 were foreign-language parishes, including the first to be founded for Mexicans—Our Lady of Guadalupe in 1920. Three Italian-language parishes were established between 1919 and 1927, but two served an English-speaking population as well. Italians were still the group least likely to give strong support to an ethnic parish.

Bishop Gallagher gave permission in 1927 for the establishment of a second parish for Detroit's black Catholics, the first, St. Peter Claver founded in 1911. It was not that the numbers of black Catholics in the city warranted a second parish (their numbers were in fact very small) but that Bishop Gallagher had adopted a black seminarian for his diocese.

When Fr. Norman Dukette was ordained in 1926—the first black priest to serve in the diocese—he was asked to undertake what was essentially missionary work among Detroit's growing population of southern black migrants. The young priest could not be assigned to St. Peter Claver's parish. It had been from the first in the care of the Holy Ghost Fathers, and Bishop Gallagher was unwilling to assign a black priest to a white congregation. St. Benedict the Moor parish was the first fruits of Fr. Dukette's long career."[6]

"St. Benedict the Moor Parish was established in 1927 as the second African American parish in Detroit, and Fr. Norman Dukette was the founding pastor. In 1929, the Holy Ghost Fathers took over the parish, and Fr. Dukette became pastor of a Christ the King Parish in Flint, Michigan. The reassignment was obviously punitive although there is nothing in the archives to shed light on his offense. He was sent to Flint never to return to Detroit, where he spent the rest of his career quietly building a large and active parish."[7]

"In 1964, when St. George's Parish closed, the archbishop transferred the administration of St. Benedict the Moor parish to the Josephites, and Fr. Patrick Veal continued his ministry in Detroit as the first Josephite pastor of the parish. The plant consisted of the original church, which had been purchased in 1927, a school built in 1951, a convent that housed the Sisters of Notre Dame who staffed the school, and a rectory. A Report for 1964 listed a congregation of 600 people and 127 students in the school.

In 1964, Rev. Donald Clark was ordained a priest for the Archdiocese of Detroit. He was the first native-born Black Detroiter to serve as a diocesan priest. He was baptized at St. Benedict the Moor in 1952.

By 1969, St. Benedict's School consolidated with three other Catholic schools in the area. The last Josephite pastor, Fr. Charles Moffatt, a native of Detroit, remodeled the vacated school building, converting the first floor into a temporary chapel and the second floor to serve as a rectory. The school building became the new parish church and center in 1971.

During Fr. Veale's administration, additional property was acquired close by for a proposed new church. In 1971, the old church and rectory was sold to a Baptist congregation. Construction began in the spring, and the new church was dedicated on September 12, 1971.

In 1973, after an extensive self-study analysis of the parish was conducted, the Josephite Council decided to return the administration of St. Benedict's Parish to the Archdiocese of Detroit. This decision was due to the insufficient man power for society commitments and the isolation of the Detroit mission from other Josephite missions. On October 6, 1973, the parish was turned over to a diocesan administrator. During the nine years as a Josephite parish, St. Benedict's had a total of 182 baptisms, of which 98 were converts."[8]

Phyllis Cobb, a former member of St. Benedict's, came to Presentation—Our Lady of Victory parish after the closing. She has been the assistant organist for a number of years until sidelined by illness. She was a member of The Society of the Little Flower, part of the group who kept things moving at St. Benedict the Moor.

Sources

1. "Our History." Article. Presentation Church Archives. 4 March 2004.

2. "4-Bedroom, 2 Bath Homes Now Available." *The Michigan Catholic*. Editorial. 12 August 1954: 13.

3. "In Our Opinion: Whites' Mass-Movement Deflates Home Values." Editorial. *The Michigan Catholic*. 13 August 1953: 4.

4. *Afro-American and Catholic: Growth and Service,* comp. and ed., Institute for Continuing Education (Detroit: Archdiocese of Detroit, 1975) 32, 33.

5. ———*The Second Generation of Mission Churches.* 29

6. Leslie Woodcock Tentler, *Seasons of Grace: The Gallagher and Mooney Episcopates.* (Wayne State University Press: Detroit, Michigan, 1994). 307.

7. ———*Catholics in a Changing World.* 505.

8. Peter Hogan. St. Joseph's Society of the Sacred Heart Archives. Maryland.

Epilogue

There is no evidence to suggest that the Catholic Church played a prominent role in the lives of the black Catholics in the Detroit area, and when it did, somehow the black churches ended up closing. It's OK to want to belong to your own ethnic-specific parish. The problem lies in the fact that the archdiocese did not give black churches the same level of support that the other ethnic churches received.

The biggest obstacle was labeling these churches missions and assigning administrators instead of pastors. This label far outlived its usefulness when the churches no longer qualified as missions, as if they ever did! Labels can impact lives negatively or positively, and one must be careful in the use of them.

What happened at St. Benedict the Moor is a lesson in what not to do if you want a church to survive. They had a black priest and sent him to Flint. Whatever happened did not justify this action when black priests were in short supply. After constructing a brand-new church, it closed a couple years later.

Holy Ghost had a black assistant priest that should have been groomed to take over that parish. To add insult to injury, Holy Ghost finally got a new church constructed on top of a foundation that sat incomplete for years, and then it closes its doors soon after.

St. George has a large membership and the Home Visitors of Mary to assist in growing that parish. The Chrysler Freeway project slates it for demolition. A pattern emerges for all to see.

Our Lady of Victory was victimized because of a control issue between the Franciscan Order and the Archdiocese of Detroit. All of these churches had missionary priests, and archdiocesan personnel took over all of them. A pattern emerges for all to see.

The vision was all wrong. The archdiocese was not focused on grooming the black church for its own ethnic priests. Blacks were the only group to have priests from different ethnic backgrounds, and it simply did not work.

Thanks for the missionary priest's presence in the black church. But even the missionaries didn't go far enough to get young boys to consider the priesthood or young girls to consider religious life. The Holy Ghost Fathers gave the diocese its second black priest. The Archdiocese of Detroit did produce two local black priests. But between the diocese and the missionary priests, black churches lost considerable ground in building their own pastoral leadership. Fr. Alvin Deem of the Franciscan Order didn't get to finish what he started.

Once you learn the history of the early pioneers of Our Lady of Victory, a pattern starts to emerge. Just about all of them quietly left Our Lady of Victory and moved on to other parishes or other denominations. Sometimes whole families picked up and left.

Former OLV members have gone on to Protestant churches that accepted them. Others who were candidates for the priesthood or religious life dropped out of sight. We know now that young boys were routinely rejected from the seminary. It leaves you wondering why when you see what is happening in the black church today.

The other pattern is that OLV parishioners were members of the Knights and Ladies of St. Peter Claver Council and Court and continued their affiliations as they moved to other parishes. Often they became the leaders in those parishes. Now some of those parishes have merged and closed or are in the process of closing. Our Lady of Victory suffered the loss of each one of those parishioners, and it took its toll on this historic church.

The clustered parishes today have a pastor, not an administrator. By contrast, Presentation—Our Lady of Victory parish is holding its own after completing its merger and going through many administrators. Some folks don't like the term *cluster*. I do not like the term *administrator* because of what it has come to mean to me.

Hopefully, we can take comfort in knowing that we are not alone in the struggle for our spiritual life. Other black churches have suffered the same fate. At least we will have some kind of history to pass on to our children, so they will learn and never forget what has happened.

APPENDIX

Some Interesting Facts

In 1951, Our Lady of Victory Church Bulletin had six pages of articles and happenings usually found in large parishes.

On January 27, 1952, Reverend Mr. Hubert Michael Sanders was baptized at Our Lady of Victory and was named after Fr. Hubert Roberge.

St. Augustine's Messenger was created to make the work of the Catholic Church among blacks better known, and to raise money to aid the cause for which the Society of the Divine Word (SVD) missionaries were working ... more black priests and religious.

Black Catholics were not admitted to seminaries or Catholic universities in the United States, because that was the custom of the land even though they have been a part of Catholicism as far back as the sixteenth century in this country (*In the Beginning.* Reprint U.S. Catholic. Apr 1993).

The original founder of the city of Chicago, Illinois, was a black Catholic trader and trapper named John Baptiste du Sable (www.holyangels.com/BlackCath.htm).

Fr. Tyrone Robinson, former administrator of OLV, was inspired to be a priest at eight years old when he walked inside St. George Church and had a strong urge to do what he saw the priest do at the altar, and he was not yet Catholic.

Luther C. Keith was a member of the United Committee on Negro History that was responsible for establishing Black History Month, and Luther A. Keith, his son, wrote a tribute to him that appeared in the *Detroit News Michigan Magazine* on February 23, 1986.

Royal Oak Township once stretched as far north as Troy Township, Greenfield Township to the south in Wayne county, to the east by Warren Township in Macomb County, and to the west by Southfield Township.

Fr. Thomas Ebong, resident priest at Our Lady of Good Counsel, Detroit, was instrumental in helping the Home Visitors of Mary establish their ministry at the Federal Capital of Nigeria where he had connections and where life was comparable to the United States in terms of basic amenities.

October 7 is the feast of Our Lady of Victory.

Sr. Virginie Fish, OSP who taught at Our Lady of Victory School, is the head of the Mother Mary Lange Guild whose mandate is to promote the <u>Cause of Beatification and Canonization</u> of <u>Mother Mary Lange, OSP</u>.

Terms and Definitions

Acolytes. A term for altar boys.

ADF. Archdiocesan Development Fund (Now Catholic Services Appeal CSA).

Cluster. Two or more merged parishes with one pastor as the head. History and identity is intact. It was called a merger when Presentation and Our Lady of Victory combined in the seventies, and both parishes lost its history and identity.

Cooperative Housing. An enterprise or organization that is owned or managed jointly by those who use its facilities or services. Royal Oak Township residents were pioneers in this concept, which allows for affordable housing.

Duns Scotus. Seminary in Southfield that was home to the Franciscan Friars. It was sold to Word of Faith Church.

DSR. The Department of Streets and Railways (Now called DDOT). Provided bus service for the Detroit region and also a chartered bus to take the children of OLV to Madonna and St. Paul School on Oakman Boulevard in Detroit.

Homily. A sermon or piece of writing on a moral or religious topic.

Investiture. Installation [into the priesthood]; inauguration.

Laity. Lay people rather than clergy.

Mangle. A machine for ironing laundry by passing it between heated rollers. Used to clean the nuns' garments.

Oakdale Gardens subdivision. A small tract of land in Royal Oak Township having the status of a unit of local government with varying governmental powers.

Sanguine. Confident; hopeful; bloodthirsty.

Sodality Deanery. A devotional or charitable society for the laity in the Roman Catholic Church. Each deanery is divided by parishes (now called the

Vicariate). *Deanery* is a term used to define the territorial jurisdiction of an ecclesiastical dean.

Vatican II. The Catholic Church entered into the new Liturgy with Mass in English, with Sunday Masses facing the people, with processions of the Bible, and with the offering of the bread and wine to the priest by the ushers of the Mass. Under the leadership of the Holy Name Men in the year of 1964 at OLV, Alfred Cook of the ushers committee and Razz Flowers of the readers committee implemented the new participation.

West Eight Mile Community. Development of black Royal Oak Township, divided between east and west by Wyoming and sandwiched between the cities of Oak Park and Ferndale on the border of West Eight Mile Road to the north of a small black community in Detroit.

List of Pastors and Administrators

Presentation Pastors

1941–1956 The Rev. Thomas. McMahon
1956–1969 The Rev. Stanley Shafer

Our Lady Of Victory Administrators

1943–1946 The Rev. Alvin Deem, OFM
1947–1953 The Rev. Hubert Roberge
1953–1959 Msgr. Ferdinand DeCnuedt
1959–1962 The Rev. Raymond Maiburger
1962–1965 The Rev. Walter Bracken
1965–1967 The Rev. Edward O'Grady
1967–1970 The Rev. Joseph Ferrens

Presentation—Our Lady Of Victory Administrators

1970–1973 Msgr. Thomas Finnegan
1973–1975 The Rev. Jerome Fraser
1975–1981 The Rev. Richard Hartmann*; **
1981–1983 The Rev. Donald Archambault
1983–1985 The Rev. Edward Waters
1985–1989 The Rev. Tyrone Robinson
1989–1992 The Rev. Joseph Gagnon
1992–1994 The Rev. Randall Phillips
1994–1995 The Rev. Ronald Rhodes
1995–1999 The Rev. Kenneth Stuart
1999–2000 The Rev. Edward Scheurman
2000–2003 The Rev. Donald Archambault***
2003—Present The Rev. Mr. Hubert Sander

* *Fr. Patrick Halfpenny served in 1977 with Fr. Hartmann.*
***Update from the Catholic Directory of the Archives. Archdiocese of Detroit. 4, 1977.*
****The church became a three-parish cluster: Presentation—OLV, IHM, and St. Gerard. The parish approved Fr. Don Archambault's return. When he left, the parish was removed from the cluster.*

List of Pioneers

Josef Baker Family*
Mother Anna Bates*
Uly McGill Brooks
Jean Sharpe Brooks*
Fred and Almeta Carruth*
Claude* and Marcella Carter
The Castleberry Family
The Bud* and Darlie Bouie Family
The DuPlessis-Ward Family
Cleo Johnson Ellis
The Ford Family
Betty Palmer-Fulgium*
Conrad C. Gordon
The Rosa-Green Family
Princess Sharpe Howard
Steve and Audrey Johnson*
The Laird Family
The Thomas Lester Family
Mary Sears and Geraldine Palmer-Long*
Dora Lowman
Vincent McGill*
The McKenzie Family
Dora Johnson Moore
Betty White-Palmer
Rosetta Palmer*
Riley Queen
Antonio and Mary Rosa*
The Sears Family
Sr. Mary Schultz
The Clothilde Smith Family
Marlene DuPlessis-Talley
Joyce Sharpe Vaughn*
Doc Washington*
Roland Webbs
Evelyn Johnson-Williams
Almeta Carruth-White
Foster and Earline Wilson Sr.*
The Young Family (Sr. Sharon Young, OSP)

Deceased
Source: *The Golden Jubilee of Fr. Alvin Deem Souvenir Book.*

List of Oblate Sisters of Providence

Sister Mary Alpsonsa Spears, OSP**
Sister Mary Amadeus Hancock, OSP (Deceased)
Sister Mary Andrew Booker, OSP**
Sister Mary Angela Wade, OSP (Deceased)
Sister Mary Angelica Wilson, OSP
Sister Mary Anita Johnson, OSP**
Sister Mary Antonio Spruell, OSP (Deceased)**
Sister Mary Augustine Greene, OSP
Sister Mary Bernardo Butler, OSP
Sister Mary Bridget Roberson, OSP**
Sister Mary Canisius Hansberry, OSP**
Sister Mary Celine McTaggart, OSP (Deceased)
Sister Mary Charlotte Marshall, OSP
Sister Mary Cleophus Carroll, OSP (Deceased)
Sister Mary Concetta Melton, OSP
Sister Mary Cyprian Jones, OSP (Deceased)
Sister Mary David Smallwood, OSP (Deceased)
Sister Mary DePaul Yancy, OSP
Sister Mary Dolorita Atwell, OSP**
Sister Mary Dushene Banks, OSP (Deceased)
Sister Mary Eileen Marino, OSP
Sister Mary Emma Haddrick, OSP (Deceased)
Sister Mary Francine Johnson, OSP (Deceased)
Sister Mary Gabriel Walker, OSP*
Sister Mary Marie Infanta Gonzales, OSP (Deceased)
Sister Mary Jacinta Broscoe, OSP* (Deceased)
Sister Mary Jacqueline Moseby, OSP
Sister Mary Katharine Brent, OSP*
Sister Mary Margaretta Bell, OSP (Deceased)
Sister Mary Marsha Marshall, OSP**
Sister Mary Mathew Patton, OSP**
Sister Mary Maureen Jones, OSP (Deceased)
Sister Mary Nathaniel Jackson, OSP (Deceased)
Sister Mary of Nazareth Johnson, OSP (Deceased)
Sister Mary Patricia Ford, OSP (Deceased)
Sister Mary Providencia Pollard, OSP**

Sister Mary Rita Michelle Proctor, OSP
Sister Mary Miriam Rogers, OSP (Deceased)
Sister Mary Sharon Young, OSP*
Sister Mary Stella Marie Harris, OSP (Deceased)
Sister Mary Stephana Smith, OSP (Deceased)
Sister Mary Stephen Beauford, OSP*
Sister Mary Teresita Thomas, OSP (Deceased)
Sister Mary Thomasine Moore, OSP**
Sister Mary Trinita Beaza, OSP
Sister Mary Vianney Wair, OSP*
Sister Mary Vincentia Randall, OSP (Deceased)
Sister Mary Virginie Fish, OSP
Sister Mary Zoila Sifontes, OSP (Deceased)

Served at Presentation
**Alive but no longer Oblates, Called Cojourners*
Revised December 2003

List of Organizations

1. Knights of St. Peter Claver Santa Maria Council #105
2. Ladies Auxiliary Knights of Peter Claver
3. Rosary and Altar Society
4. The Legion of Mary
5. League of Catholic Women
6. Carmelite Third Order
7. St. Joseph Society
8. Our Lady of Victory Choral Club
9. Our Lady of Victory Girl Scouts
10. Our Lady of Victory Boy Scouts (since 1949)
11. The Sacred Heart Study Club
12. Our Lady of Fatima Study Club
13. St. Rita's Study Club
14. Altar Boys Society
15. Ushers Club
16. St. Vincent DePaul Society
17. Junior and Senior Sodality of Our Lady
18. Holy Name Society of Men
19. Oblate Sisters of Providence Guild
20. CYO Teen Club
21. Our Lady of Victory Credit Union
22. PTA

These clubs were all openly seeking new members and were very active.

Knights of St. Peter Claver Santa Maria Council #105

Date: Established February 6, 1949
Area Deputy: Luther C. Keith, Northern District Organizer
Name of Church: Our Lady of Victory Mission
Pastor: Rev. Hubert Roberge
Chartered Members: Council-50; Court-17
Grand Lady: Ruth Rosa Green-Leonard
Grand Knight: Fred Carruth

Our Lady of Victory—Presentation Council/Court #189

Reestablishment Date: February 19, 1977
Area Deputy: Willie Kelley—Council; Annie Rosemond—Court
Name of Church: Presentation—Our Lady of Victory
Pastor: Rev. Richard Hartmann
Chartered Members: Council-12; Court-18 (see next page)
Grand Lady: Helen Wilson
Grand Knight: Foster Wilson Jr.
Junior Knights: Branch Mother—Denise Sears
Junior Daughter Counselor: Jackie Blakely; Assistant—Betty Fulgiam

Court 189 Chartered Members

Betty Jean Bradley (Deceased)

Helen Hill (Deceased)

Geraldine Long (Deceased)

Jacqueline Long

Lorna Welsh

Zenobia Manning

Mary Maurant

Rosetta Palmer

Georgia Lowe

Erma Hodges

Evelyn Perdue

Dolores Anderson

Margaret Reese

Helen Wilson (Deceased)

Billie Sue Merritt

Doris M. Robinson

Christine Roberts

Rev. Richard Hartmann, pastor

Sodality of Our Lady of Victory

Name	Date of Reception
1. Betty Palmer	1947
2. Mary Palmer	1947
3. Freddie Brown	1947
4. Marie Bates	1947
5. Florence Ward	1947
6. Marlene Ward	1947
7. Valivia Byron	1949 (May)
8. Betty White	1949
9. Geraldine Palmer	1949
10. Yvonne Wilson	1947
11. Beth Wilson	1947
12. Dolores Robinson	1947
13. Almeta Carruth	1947
14. Alice Hines	1947
15. Henrietta Barksdale	1947
16. Dolores Young	1947
17. Barbara Carter	1951 (December)
18. Betty Hunnicutt	1951 (December)
19. Barbara Hodges	1951 (December)
20. Shirley Lenier	1951 (December)
21. Jean Smith	1951 (December)
22. Betty Leonard	1951 (December)
23. Thelma Laird	1951 (December)
24. Alta Ruth Laird	1951 (December)
25. Beverly Castleberry	1951 (December)
26. Veronica Ward	1951 (December)

The Sodality Record Book was supplied by Betty White-Palmer.

CYO Teen Club

Ratification of Officers

Jerry Rankin, president
Pamela Cox, vice president
Connie Heard, secretary
Tom Cook, treasurer

Committee Chairmen

Daryl Robinson, Spiritual Committee
Rosalin Young, Social Committee
Beatrice Gray, Civic-Cultural Committee
Frank Graves, Athletic Committee

Credit Union Directors and Committees
January 1952

Board of Directors

Fr. Hubert Roberge
Eaton Metoyer
Thomas Lester
James Anderson
Hattie Braddock
Margaret Carter

Supervisory Committee

Gladys Oldham
Ardell Walker
Lawson Conway

Committee

William McDonald
Claude Carter
John Luckett

Rosary/Altar Society Committees
January 11, 1962

President: Bette Flowers   **Treasurer:** Viola Wilkins

Vice President: Ruth Little   **Secretary:** Glodene Spight

Altar: Chairman Mary Fuller with the Junior Girls Legion of Mary

Linen: Chairman Louise Thomas; Co-Chairman Catherine Sumpter

Kitchen: Lillie Leonard supported by ladies of the parish

Special Dinners and Refreshments: Chairman Darlie Bouie supported by Sodality Girls

Spiritual Development: Chairman Mary E. Robinson

Sick: Mary Maison

Membership Hostess: Glodene Spight, Joyce Giles, Loretta Whitely, C. Hylton, and Barbara Cushione

Volunteers: Chairman Audrey Johnson; Co-Chairman E. Willis

League of Catholic Women: E. Wilson

Parish Contact: Viola Wilkins

Publicity: Chairman: Brenda Sumpter

Sewing Projects: Chairman Ruth Little; Co-Chair Thelma Rankin

Entertainment: Chairman Laura Smith; Co-Chair Frances Johnson

The Festival Committee
June 24, 1962

Raffle Ticket Returns Committee

James Lovelace
Steve Johnson
Washington Leonard

Booths Run by the Ladies

Linen and Apron Booth: Chairman Ruth Little, Co-Chair Thelma Rankin
Country Store and Bake Sale: Lillie Leonard, Minnie Johnson
White Elephant Booth: Earline Wilson, Laura Smith
Chicken Dinner: Darlie Bouie
Refreshments: Doris West
Cashiers: Thelma Horn, Mary Doctor

Booths Run by the Men

Cigarette Booth
Penny Pitch
Milk Bottles
Las Vegas Games
Duck Pond
Hula Hoop
Prizes: $1,000 cash
Portable TV
FM Radio
Portable Record Player

978-0-595-43482-4
0-595-43482-7

Made in the USA
Monee, IL
06 October 2020